PN Review 237

VOLUME 44   NUMBER 1   SEPTEMBER–OCTOBER

REPORTS ——————————

REVIEWS ——————————

POEMS ——————————

FEATURES ——————————

ON THE COVER
Eugenia Loli, *Summer Dreams* (collage, 2012).
Cover curator: Valgerður Þóroddsdóttir.

Editorial

On 30 July Philip Pullman, president of the Society of Authors, galvanized writers, independent publishers and booksellers. He called for the re-introduction of a minimum price for books, in effect the restoration of the Net Book Agreement, which was declared illegal by the Restrictive Practices Court in March 1997. At that time it had been in force from 1 January 1900.

Older readers may experience a sense of déjà vu. *PN Review* 68 and 69 (1989) featured NBA editorials, as did 106 and 109 (1995–96); it was a subject of correspondence and figured in News and Notes. Pullman, a clear-headed spokesman for writers and literary provision, was keen to protect what remains of the beleaguered independent bookshops. He dubbed them 'the lantern bearers of civilisation', a charming archaism: the bookshop as Diogenes in search of an honest man. The Booksellers' Association welcomed his suggestion; the Publishers' Association, dominated by the big players, didn't.

'There is an insane, inhumane and perverted belief,' Pullman said, 'that the market knows best, and that it is something natural, like gravity, which we can do nothing to alter. But of course we can alter the way the market works. It's a human construction.' He knows whereof he speaks, being a best-selling author: the independent booksellers are suffering from the heavy discounting, on pre-orders, of his forthcoming *La Belle Sauvage*, the first in the Book of Dust series, due out on 19 October from Penguin Random House and David Fickling Books. The book is officially priced at £20 but Amazon, Tesco, W.H. Smith, Waterstones and Foyles are selling it at half price, less indeed than the independent bookseller would have to pay to get stock in. They cannot afford to compete; and what is more, the author pays because his royalties will be calculated on net receipts rather than the recommended retail price.

Small booksellers for the last twenty years have been at an increasing disadvantage. Independent publishers, too, whose best-sellers are few and far between, have been brutalised by a book trade in which the large players demand discount as a condition of purchase. And the author suffers, too. Shortly before Philip Pullman made his call, chief executive of the Society of Authors Nicola Solomon – one hopes there is a whiff of collusion here – wrote to publishers urging them to eschew special sales at 'ultra-high' discounts which impact on author royalties and on the market as a whole.

One major change over the last two decades is the growth of online websites abroad such as Amazon from which UK customers might secure discounted books in editions published abroad. Tom Godfray of the Booksellers' Association noted how 'The NBA collapsed in the year Amazon was formed in Seattle. Any new arrangement would have to cope with the internet age, and globalisation of publishing and bookselling.' But the head of the Publishers Association, Stephen Lotinga, ruled out any change to trading terms, instead suggesting that the booksellers lobby for a reduction in business rates. In the trade this is called 'passing the book'. He talked about 'a level playing field in the book retail market'. On his level playing field, one bookseller gets 70 percent discount, another 35 percent.

The European Commission does not forbid retail price maintenance on books. France, Germany, Italy, the Netherlands and Spain enjoy this protection and Belgium is on the verge of re-introducing it. Way back in *PN Review* 192 (2010) Iain Bamforth wrote, 'Curiously, the French themselves attempted, in the late 1970s, to repeal fixed prices in the interests of encouraging competition. After two years of turmoil, during which publishers were prohibited from even recommending prices, lists were slashed, and many small independent booksellers went to the wall, a law was introduced in 1982 by Jack Lang, the then culture minister, to regulate the market. Even the French Consumers Union agreed that the free trade in books had led to a marked disparity between cities and towns, where the same book often cost more. The key paradox: 'Price freedom was undemocratic. France – and most EU countries for that matter – therefore still apply the continental form of the Net Book Agreement, which obliges retailers to sell books at agreed prices (Amazon is able to discount titles by only 5 percent in France).'

May Philip Pullman's arguments prevail. As Tim Waterstone declared in 1989, 'Books *are* different'. And Sir Basil Blackwell that same year wrote in the *Guardian*, 'It is the pluralism of book publishing that gives it its joy and strength, and this pluralism is protected by the fact that the publisher and bookseller are able to provide a market place for minority titles at stable prices and stable profit margins.' Sir Simon Hornby, then chairman of W.H. Smith, championed the NBA. *PN Review* declared in those dark days, and declares again in these, 'Success and efficiency can be variously measured: even in an age obsessed with margins and stock turn, they can relate to specialism, or to benefiting specific communities. Some booksellers may try to give excellent service, costly to the bottom line for single-copy and special orders. Some make substantial cultural contributions on tiny margins. Bookselling might still be a service *as well as* a business. The margins that spell the difference between survival and extinction are sustained by the NBA.' All strength to Philip Pullman's elbow.

News & Notes

Second Collections · Sandeep Parmar's *Eidolon*, published by Shearsman Books, has been awarded the inaugural Ledbury Forte Poetry Prize, the UK's first prize dedicated to *second* poetry collections, and worth £5,000. The judges were Vahni Capildeo and Tara Bergin. Vahni writes about the judging process in this issue of PNR.

Homer in Sicily · At the end of the nineteenth century Samuel Butler proposed that the *Odyssey* was written by a woman living in Trapani, Sicily, thus placing himself squarely in the millennium-long debate on the location of the events narrated by the Homeric poems. To find evidence for his theory, Butler visited Sicily many times during the last ten years of his life. His studies took an anthropological direction. He took a significant collection of photographs across the island. The Fardelliana Library, in partnership with the St John's College Library in Cambridge, has organised a photographic exhibition and an international conference titled 'Samuel Butler's Route: Geographies and Anthropologies into the *Odyssey*'. The conference is taking place on the 27th of September, in Trapani, and features three guest speakers: Dr Edith Hall (King's College London), Dr Elinor Shaffer (University of London) and Dr Cristiano Turbil (King's College London). The exhibition will open to the public the following spring at the Specus Corallii, located in the historic centre of Trapani.

First Translation Prize · Translator Daniel Hahn has donated half his winnings from the 2017 International Dublin Literary Award to establish a new prize for debut literary translation – the Translators' Association's First Translation Prize, which will be run by the Society of Authors. The award is also backed by the British Council: 'It aims to recognise excellent debut literary prose translation published in the UK, and will be shared between the first-time translator and her/his editor.' Further details will be published in due course.

Poet Laureate · The Librarian of Congress Carla Hayden has announced the appointment of Princeton University professor Tracy K. Smith as the Library's 22nd Poet Laureate Consultant in Poetry, for 2017–18. She will take up her duties in the autumn, opening the Library of Congress's annual literary season with a reading of her work. Hayden said of Smith's work, 'it travels the world and takes on its voices; brings history and memory to life; calls on the power of literature as well as science, religion and pop culture'. Smith was awarded the Pulitzer Prize for Poetry in 2012. She succeeds Juan Felipe Herrera as poet laureate.

Griffin · Alice Oswald's *Falling Awake* has been awarded the 2017 International Griffin Prize. The purse is substantial, in sterling terms £37,725. The same sum was also presented to the Vancouver poet Jordan Abel, who received the Canadian prize with his long poem about cultural appropriation and racism, *Injun*.

Helen Dunmore · The poet, historical novelist, story and children's writer Helen Dunmore died in June. She was sixty-four. She was one of Bloodaxe Books' first writers, publishing her first collection, *The Apple Fall*, in 1983. Bloodaxe remained her poetry publisher. Her latest (tenth) collection, *Inside the Wave*, appeared in April. She published twelve novels and three books of short stories with Penguin, including *A Spell of Winter* (1995), winner of the Orange Prize for Fiction, and four novels with Hutchinson. She also wrote sixteen books for children and eight for young adults. Her poetry publisher Neil Astley will contribute a memoir to a later issue of *PNR*.

Your more secret mind · The Jamaican poet James Berry, who by bringing Patois to British poetry so successfully destabilised and opened it out, has died. He was ninety-two. He arrived in Britain in 1948, after six years in the United States, settling in Brixton. Racism and poverty contributed to his early poetry. He joined the Caribbean Artists Movement early, along with Kamau Brathwaite, Wilson Harris, Andrew Salkey, George Lamming, Samuel Selvon, Stuart Hall and his publisher John La Rose. His first poetry book, *Fractured Circles*, was published in 1979 by New Beacon Books. In 1981 he was awarded the National Poetry prize for 'Fantasy of an African Boy'. He declared, 'Poems come from your more secret mind. A poem will want to ask deeper questions, higher questions, more puzzling questions, and often too, more satisfying questions than the everyday obvious questions...' He edited two key, questioning anthologies, *Bluefoot Traveller* (1976) and *News for Babylon* (1984), and indefatigably championed West Indian/British writing. In 1990 he was appointed to the Order of the British Empire. His *Selected Poems*, under the title *A Story I am In*, was published by Bloodaxe in 2011.

Burnt matchsticks · Another leading Bloodaxe poet, the Russian dissident Irina Ratushinskaya, a survivor of four years in the Gulag, died in Moscow in July. She was sixty-three. She composed 250 poems under detention, some committed to memory in the manner of Akhmatova's poems, some scratched with burnt matchsticks into bars of soap. 'When I finished, I would memorize it, wash my hands and send it down the drain,' she said. Transcribed on cigarette papers, they found their way via her husband to the West. Human rights groups took up her cause and worked for her freedom which at last came in 1986, one of the first fruits of *glasnost*, shortly before Presidents Gorbachev and Reagan were due to meet in Reykjavik. Bloodaxe published *No, I'm Not Afraid* in that year, to great acclaim. She and her husband had Russian citizenship restored under Yeltsin, moving to Moscow in 1998 so that their children could be educated in Russian schools.

Eunice de Souza · Poet, teacher, novelist and journalist Eunice de Souza has died in Mumbai at the age of seventy-six. The poets she taught and inspired, principally women writers, found her example and approach liberating. Her first book of poems, *Fix*, was published in 1979, and focused on the Goan Catholics living in Mumbai. Her most recent, *Learn from the Almond Leaf*, last year. Her two novels, *Dangerlok* (2001) and *Dev and Simran* (2003), expanded on her poetic work, using colloquial Bandra English, giving it literary legitimacy. She was also a great advocate through her important anthology work, including *Nine Indian Women Poets*, *101 Folktales From India*, *Women's Voices: Selections from Nineteenth and Early Twentieth Century Indian Writing in English* and *Early Indian Poetry in English*.

Unexpected depths · Chana Bloch, a poet and an acclaimed translator of Hebrew poetry, died in Berkeley, California, in May at the age of seventy-seven. Bloch rooted her own poetry in the work of Dickinson, Bishop and Akhmatova; the seeming simplicity was hard-earned, and her subject matter, the dailiness of family life, growing old, is connected by deft allusion to the larger stories, myths and legends provided by the Bible and other books held in common. 'I like poetry that appears to be clear on the surface, with unexpected depths.' She was a key translator of the work of Israeli poets Dahlia Ravikovitch and Yehuda Amichai.

Pakistan · The celebrated Urdu poet and writer Hasan Akbar Kamal died in July in Karachi. He was seventy-one. Like Euncie de Souza, he was a significant teacher as well as a leading figure in the literature of Pakistan in the years after Partition. He started writing young and his songs became well known before he died. He wrote several collections of poetry, a book of essays, and he also wrote for children.

The Blond Beast · Heathcote Williams, who has died at the age of seventy-five, was a poet of aggravated temper, a playwright, humourist, activist and actor. His most durable contributions may be to the cause of environmental issues, addressed in some of his most effectively polemical work. An old Etonian, one of his last gestures was to assault Boris Johnson with *The Blond Beast of Brexit: a Study in Depravity* (2016). In the late 1980s he wrote *Whale Nation*, a celebration and a plea for the preservation of the giant mammal, *Sacred Elephant*, which took the theme further, and *Autogeddon*, which in ballad form attacks the car and what it does to land and life. Horatio Morpurgo sent *PNR* a poem in memory of Williams:

The night I heard that Heathcote Williams was gone
I had planned to work and even tried but no use.
Walking through town at dusk on a midsummer Sunday –
 Streets and bars all but deserted –
Some subconscious trail led me to water.
It stood me at last on a little bridge
Between an old factory still in use, turning out
High-spec cables for half the world's military –
I always smile –
Even its alarm system is called Real World Services –
The people they flew in from Sri Lanka to install it
Cycled around town for a few weeks then vanished –
On a little road bridge between all of that
And a housing estate, I leant upon a brick parapet
And noted as night fell how severely, year by year,
They cut back the river-side vegetation where I saw an otter
 once.
Under an escort of its own blue lights, as I meditated on
 this,
An ambulance passed down West Street in silence and in no
 hurry
Then turned along the narrow street towards where I stood.
The pulsing of its light grew stronger, started reflecting
In the windows of the houses and parked cars, cast even
A blue flicker among the leaves and shadows of the trees
Right along the dark line of our ill-used river.
The silhouette of a gull floated above as that ambulance
Followed the road round and went out of sight.

On Judging Prizes, and Reading More than Six Really Good Books

VAHNI CAPILDEO

JUDGING THE LEDBURY FORTE PRIZE, which awards £5,000 to the author of a second collection of poetry, inspired me to search a property website. I selected 'London', 'one bedroom apartment' (assuming a second-collection poet might need to fit in another person as well as themselves, a desk and some books). The listings hit £500 per month – for shared flats or houses of multiple occupation. What looks like a great lump of cash is not even a year's rent.

Prizes are not income. They cannot be relied upon. What can be relied upon is the opprobrium which judging attracts. Here are some answers. You can write the questions.

(a) Agitate for writing to be recognised as labour. If you do lots of stuff for free for your mates because art is lovely and the system is fucked – this, too, is an exercise of economic agency, with consequences. Less whinge, more *manifestation à la française*. Are you participating in local politics, or co-ordinating public interventions (leafleting, graffiti, digital...)? Applying to Teach First or the civil service? Join the Society of Authors. Read www.gov.uk guidelines for freelancers.

(b) There is no 'prize culture'. There are numerous, interlinked, imperfect mechanisms for bringing more, and different, poetry to more, and different readers – including those outside these four nations, who nonetheless happen (who knows why?) to read in English.

(c) If your publisher did not enter your book, it was not considered. Speak to your publisher. You might know that some prizes require thousands of pounds in fees. Do you know your own publisher's overheads? Could they enter, win, and survive?[1]

Cast the Amazon Prime subscription out of thy debits before casting the 'prize' books off your reading list. Ask the Poetry Book Society, or your preferred book club, about their policy on the discounts they want from publishers, and what 'sweeteners' they expect regarding review copies and returns. Get the figures. Do not rest content with a sucralose answer.

Do not hint reproachfully to judges about the merits of your friends above that lucky, pretty girl, or that smooth, privileged guy. Do not corner me in the pub; I am somewhat Glaswegian.

Naturally, the poetry prize judging process consists in leisurely discussion in the enforced luxury of an unnamed resort, while beautiful robots convert conversation to digital notes. Alternatively, for evil awards, black gowned judges throw books around, roaring with scorn, and pick the winner via perverted party games.

In fact, here were my material conditions of judging. A major worry was receiving the books (not all prizes are set up for electronic submissions). Unemployed since the end of September – winning the Forward Prize having proved a job interview-killer ('you'll be busy with your performances') – I was zigzagging for paid gigs between Ireland, Spain, London, the US and elsewhere, in an unglamorous, economy-class way – a structural, relationship-destroying instability. My Brexitish Cambridge neighbours, who had refused to introduce themselves, would not keep post. So I had to ask a favour from someone with a college address.

Two boxes of books filled my Trinidad suitcase. Luckily I have spare clothing at 'home'. I failed in Bocas Litfest attendance, staying in reading; failed my mother, alone in the next room, disabled and in pain. My hands wintergreened from the massage gel I used all too briefly on her benumbed or aching limbs. With birdsong and breezes irritatingly fulfilling tropical stereotypes beyond my closed, sea-blue curtains, I worked through sixty-two volumes.

I dedicated time to engage closely only with these books, keeping any other texts, including 'my own', at the margin of my attention. Only thus would my brain guard a fair field for comparison. I had to get beyond *what I liked* and ask, what is this doing?

Technology did not fail. My co-judge, Tara Bergin, kindly met via FaceTime. Given the time zone difference, I was in red-and-white reindeer pyjamas, and attached to a coffee mug. In a triumph for feminism, as well as for flexible working, Tara batted not an eyelid, but conversed with an efficiency that had me rethinking. One of the most exciting aspects of good judging is the back-to-school feeling. A co-judge is not a fellow seminar leader, or a new best friend. However, the deciding conversations, attentive and appetitive, urgent and generous, have a youthful feeling of both 'all the time in the world' and 'this! now!'. It was revitalising to compare personal reactions as well as other criteria; to share note-taking systems, and how much we read aloud.

We wanted 'good poetry'. We were startled when the natural distribution of our selection was apparently gender-balanced: three designated male, three designated female (we did not check how the authors identify), not London-centric, and entirely from independent presses. I feel almost as nervous about my 'judgments' as I do about my own new poems – *is this any good, or have I run mad?* – and put in just as much work. Yet there was overlap with Tara's list – both in terms of some titles, and in the kinds of thing we were looking for.

Patterns did emerge. I wonder how much the 'creative writing industry' applies a beauty treatment body-wrap, massaging out any heritage-unfriendly toxins. There was a tendency to use an imported structure, sometimes with extra pieces tacked on: x number of poems about paintings, or a scientific phenomenon, or a particular human experience. There was a worrying amount of encoded misogyny. There was a tendency to be safe: male poets often came across as nice guys, while female poets had airbrushed out inconvenient neighbours in their grieving, floral paths. Historical voices, though well-researched, were seldom as badly behaved and diverse as in records, or memories, of the 'real' past.

Personally what I found heart-breaking were the few cases when books had similar virtues but only one could be chosen rather than another. What was heartening was how many second-collection, or second-book, authors were alive to the whole world; though they might choose to work in miniatures or monologues, they showed relish and love and indignation about the absurdities of our embodied selves and the weirdness of Internetted conscious-ness cross-cutting each potentially lyric instant.

I have written often about the scope and non-interchangeability of the terms 'book' and 'collection'. A pragmatic interpretation might be best, when a well-meaning person or institution uses the terms interchangeably. Challenging assumptions and definitions is important. Challenges also need to be made well, to be heard as anything other than ornery. A 'book' has coherence, yet might not make much sense or yield its pleasures and illuminations to a reader dipping in at random. A 'collection' may have been rearranged by mentors and editors and will comprise roughly equal, publishable or performable, stand-alone pieces.

I would hope that the Ledbury Forte Prize, for a second publication, rewards the difficulty of produc-ing that object which has an ISBN can travel – across borders. It is not easy for a poet to find 'headspace'

and resist 'steering' to break away from – even if continuing – where the first publication left off. It is a fine feeling, as a judge, to be able to redistribute some resources – though not a year's London rent – to an author who shows this resilience, and whose work seems still to be responsive and evolving.

Here are the shortlisted titles, with my unedited comments from my secret Excel sheet of notes after a first reading:

Sandeep Parmar, *Eidolon* (Shearsman) – Extraordinary lens on maze-like power structure through myth, war, tech & the 'female'. [This was the winner.]
Judy Brown, *Crowd Sensations* (Seren) – Clever, attentive to material & viewpoint; also individualistic, tripping away.
John Clegg, *Holy Toledo!* (Carcanet) – Clever, with some astonishing lines.
Emma Hammond, *The Story of No* (Penned in the Margins) – Post-post-Internet smarts. Tough & moving daughter-mother elegy. Rare.
John McCullough, *Spacecraft* (Penned in the Margins) – Central lover's-death sequence powerful. Formally playful (good).
Sam Riviere, *Kim Kardashian's Marriage* (Faber & Faber) – Witty, pretty, hiding its heart; sharply concerned with the whole 'globalised' world.

There is a much longer sheet of comments, not to be given away anywhere. I suggest you read all these books instead.

NOTES
[1] See, for example, www.theguardian.com/ books/2017/jan/02/on-eve-of-costa-awards-experts- -warn-that-top-books-prizes-are-harming-fiction

---

Letter from South Korea (II)

DAVID R. MILLER

THERE IS A PROBLEM on the Korean peninsula, not necessarily a military one. It concerns the pundits who come to this place with their eyes shut, conditioned by cardboard cut-out interpretations of history. Missing from images of this peninsula are Korean voices themselves. No one even wants to lis-ten in the first place. Unreflecting commentary can betray more about the ignorance of reporters than about Korea. 'The only thing both Koreas share,' proclaimed ITV's John Irvine in April, reporting from a subway station in Seoul, 'is their last name'. As if a shared language and thousands of years of history mean nothing next to an arbitrarily demarcated partition.

To dismiss Korea as a unified territory equally dismisses the hopes of its inhabitants. Even if the younger generation cite potential economic problems as a reason to avoid reunification, there is also much evidence to the contrary. When Korea was forcibly

partitioned more negotiations were promised in nine-ty days. This never happened. The serious attempts by writers in both countries to compile a collaborative Korean dictionary are testament to a desire for this stalled reunification as much as they are signs of separation. Recently, statements like Irvine's have reached saturation point, coupled as they always are with speculative accounts of military prowess. To an active, mindful, existence here, they lend surreal qualities. There are tensions, but little justice is done by the reductions of twenty-four-hour news.

Commentary that comes from this region must pay attention to the omissions and silences. One of the most engaging pundits has been the Republican Lawrence Wilkerson, Colin Powell's chief of staff back in 2002. Wilkerson noted recently that in all of his time serving in the United States Navy's Pacific Command, it was only 'the Korean left' that ever stood up for Korean interests. Such terminology may not be particularly useful, but what Wilkerson alights on is something fundamental to any appreciation of this region. In Korea it is the North which has a detailed understanding of history, whilst intense discussions of the past only take place amongst 'dissenters' in the South. There is a fluid coalition of people in South Korea continually fighting the narrative set in place by the dictatorship. This is one reason that the desire for reunification is more palpable above the thirty-eighth parallel. Freed from the desire to explore ambiguities, the North has been able to sketch out a vision of history on its own terms.

These are the kinds of ambiguities Ko Un tried to recover in his epic *Maninbo*, where the past is dramatised via the micro histories of a previously silenced majority. What emerges from these quarters was once taboo. This includes issues such as criticism of the brutal Japanese occupation, and the collaborators that were put in place by the US Army after the Second World War. But also unimaginable injustices like the Jeju massacre on the 3 April 1948 (or 4.3 as it is commonly referred to in Korea). This is when thirty thousand people were killed as a result of an American decision (based on a complete misunderstanding of the cultural scene) that the entire island was 'red'. This history lay buried for fifty years, to even speak of it risked torture and imprisonment. From the dictatorship onwards the South Korean government used similar tactics against anyone who questioned the status quo.

This silenced history doesn't end there. What happened in Jeju was only the tip of the iceberg, and encompasses other sites across the peninsula. In South Korea there are 114 bereaved-family associations who have been in a continual fight for justice against the state. During the dictatorship they experienced sustained persecution, and even today the fight for recognition goes on. Some families in the South are still waiting to find relatives assassinated in the early stages of the Korean War under the pretext of 'communism' sixty-seven years later. The Truth and Reconciliation Commission set up in 2005 to examine this history was de-funded and effectively closed by Lee Myung Bak as soon as he came to power in 2008. Park Guen Hye repeated this pattern, continuing her father's work. Even in opposition the dictatorship class aim to keep the ledgers of history unblemished.

The same logic was explicit in Park Guen Hye's state-authorised school textbooks, which gave a ridiculously biased account of the last seventy years. There are two narratives colliding here, each of which has its own unique take on historical memory. These tensions invade every aspect of daily existence, and naturally seep into the language itself. In the North of this peninsula there is a different word for friend (동무 *dongmu*), simply because it was abandoned by the South for its associations with 'comrade' in Soviet times. This is what anyone who engages in politics has to deal with. The socio-political sphere has seen a constant recasting of old values, to position them within a less problematic context. It is why the new president of South Korea – Moon Jae In – uses the term 적폐청산 (*Jeokpye Cheongsan*, loosely translated as 'the disposal of long-standing evils') when setting out his own priorities. Any understanding of Korea

has to start with the recognition of this complexity, rather than the repetition of simplistic narratives. One of Moon Jae In's first tasks was to banish Park's state-sanctioned textbooks from the Korean classroom altogether. This Cold War logic creates subtle divisions which cannot be dealt with effectively using the same paradigms as before. Progressive political platforms must find ways to go beyond them.

A step forward was taken on the thirty-fourth anniversary of the Gwangju Uprising (1980), which took place in May, when the new president agreed to sing a song memorialising the victims. Apart from its emotional properties, this song – *March of the Beloved* – is iconic in Korea as an example of how polarised things have become. In previous years this event threatened to expose all the tensions still creeping beneath the surface. Participants could 'sing' the song but not 'chant' it, according to Park Guen Hye, because it was used in a North Korean film a long time after Gwangju itself. If you came to this ceremony last year, you would have been treated to the spectacle of half the audience stood up singing, whilst government officials sat silently in their seats. For ordinary Koreans it is scenes like these that had previously turned them off politics altogether. The still extant National Security Law (a remnant of Park Chung Hee's Yushin Constitution) simply states that 'praising the North' is banned. This is a legal framework that has often been interpreted very loosely, including a prison sentence for someone who 'retweeted' an account on Twitter associated with North Korea. Politics is a continual fight for the recognition of a place beyond this state of affairs. This is why commentary must proceed carefully, so as not to exacerbate the situation, emboldening the reactionary forces of the past. 'It is not a past we should go back to', as Ko Un writes in the aforementioned poem, 'but the start of tomorrow'.

Three Poems

ARTHUR LONGBOW

ALISTAIR ELLIOT *writes*:
Arthur Longbow was born in in 1864, briefly
attended the Slade, and died in 1940, just five years
before Symons. It seems his mother was French,
possibly one of the Languedoc Longuebeau family
– Arthur was illegitimate and perhaps this was one
of the reasons why his name was hardly known, in
spite of the quality of his verse – until one day in
the summer of 1939 his grandson George told him
they'd been reading a poem by Arthur Longbow in
the school anthology. Strange coincidence of
names, wasn't it?

THE MUSE AND I

Leaves, light cloth around limbs,
Air in the armpits and the puffy hair,
Desire rising as the firelight dims,
Both scent and powder in the atmosphere,
These are the properties we share.

We live indoors, though fond
(We say) of nature with its dirt and stings:
Under the piano you respond
With sighs as I undo the silken strings
That dash-dot-dash your cotton underthings.

THE POETS

Delicate they are,
All but transparent,
These poets, as aware
As spiders in their webs
Of the flavoursome air.

They can detect the flies,
The distant flowerbeds,
The perfumed lingeries.
They even seem to hear
The birds' amorous cries.

But don't they notice the rattle
Of death across the sea,
The approaching battle,
The wheels, the drums, the music
Of military metal?

Inside their beautiful hair
Roars the applause of art.
That is all they can hear,
No newsboys, no instruments
Of the old human choir.

Violence, theft of clothes,

Persuasion, nothing reaches
Into their dreams to dowse
The flame in their balloon:
It will continue to rise
To its beloved moon.

HOMMAGE

pour Stuart Merrill

Among the circles where my pebble fell
A lily-pad floats, balancing a frog
Who looks at me, and licks his lips. A dog
Carefully waters the wilting asphodel.
Some children watch him from their carousel,
The boys admiring and the girls agog.
Early they learn the secret dialogue
Of gender, what is beau and what is belle.

I sit back on my dark green metal bench
And watch the frog, and lick my lips. Too bad
He's safe here, public property. He flexes
His fat legs, leaning elbows on the pad.
All I can do is wonder what his sex is
And tinker with my Alexandrian French.

The American Poetry You Want

Michael & Matthew Dickman

Tuesday 14 June 2016, International Anthony Burgess Foundation, Manchester

EVAN JONES

THE BABY-FACED, AMERICAN Dickman twins rolled into Manchester on a Tuesday – and left that same Tuesday, one stop on their English-city-hopping promotional tour (London, Manchester, and a petrol station loo or two in between), touting their dual-authored Faber release, the red, white and blue *tête-bêche* (flip-book) *Brother*. It reprints poems published in individual collections by the two brothers, and it's all about their half-brother Darin, who killed himself. The Dickmans were endenimed, unbearded and wearing similar eyeglasses.

In order to tell the two brothers apart, a difficulty I have always had with identical twins, and especially because they are both wearing jeans, I list here some of the differences I noticed between them: Matthew has a bit of a squeeky voice and tatts on his arms; Michael is more nasal-voiced and may also have tatts, but his sleeves are rolled down this evening; Michael's jeans are ripped, purposefully, and his blazer is brown corduroy with a sort of superhero button on the left lapel; Matthew's jeans are rolled, his New Balance 998 Trainers are very clean, his NYC baseball cap is half-cocked (he takes the cap off for the reading, gentleman that he is, which leaves him with a bit of hathead); Michael wears green socks and a red check shirt; Matthew has a light blue dress shirt on, sleeves rolled (see above) and ankle socks; Matthew's lines are long; Michael's lines are short; Michael teaches at Princeton; Matthew is poetry editor at the American lit mag, *Tin House*; Matthew is the fun, accessible one; Michael is the serious, academic one; George is the quiet one; Ringo is the drummer.

The brothers perform together, a duo, but with their wisecracking and familial intimacy they are more the Smothers Brothers than two Beatles. Although, whenever I ask friendly poet types about the Dickmans, I hear a familiar declaration of interest in one or the other, but never both. Sort of the way Beatles fans love either John or Paul (Paul all the way, for what it's worth – John was crazy and abusive, Paul wrote the hits). Some are critical of Matthew's chattiness; some don't understand how Michael sounds anything like Emily Dickinson (a weirdly common comparison in press material). But what's Paul without John? It occurs to me, hearing them read together, talking and poeticising about Darin, that they are a double act, they inform each other, and I'm not certain Michael's poems would make sense without Matthew's.

What's sort of strange about the reading is that the poems are distressing, death-obsessed, even as the brothers keep things light with their humour and banter. Michael goes first, and describes how his poem 'Flies' developed from 'intense dreams about flies', which he had after Darin killed himself. He reads sombrely, slowly. Matthew tells us, as background to one of his poems, that he believes 'anything my twin brother tells me', and they laugh together, and the audience laughs. He reads sombrely, slowly. Before reading 'Notes Passed to My Brother on the Occasion of His Funeral', Matthew asks if we know what Costco is. We do. He says, 'I don't have to explain about a Greek god. I don't know about them. So I don't write about them.' The word 'fuck' comes up a couple times as he reads. And in-between the poems there is laughter.

Faber, their publisher, appear to have found here a poetry book with a talking point (suicide...), part of a recent flush of collections that might access an audience beyond poetry's traditional readership by being topical (that readership is, as far as I can tell, limited to between three-hundred and one thousand people per country – size of country making no difference). So *Brother* the flip-book is a gimmick. And what's wrong with a gimmick if it sells a little poetry? I hear Pound: 'Only what has been written against the market!' But the weird thing isn't the gimmick, it's the circus that comes with it. No novelist would be put through this red, white and blue nonsense. Add to this that Faber's recent American poetry list is miniscule: Kleinzahler, Seidel, Simic, not a single woman, and now the Dickman brothers sold as all-American, exotic, kind of sad but charming and pop. It's about the saleable concept, not the poems.

After the reading, asked to answer questions from the audience, the brothers talk over each other, laugh, tease, as siblings do. Michael seems more serious, Matthew more playful. Michael does most of the talking, while Matthew delivers the punch lines. An audience member wonders what they're reading. Michael responds, 'Maureen McLane and Karen Solie'; Michael lets us know he's really into *Buffy* Season Five right now (yes, the one about Dawn).

Can a Program Write a Poem?

I WAS STRUCK BY SOMETHING in a recent opinion piece in the *New York Times* by Thomas Friedman: not the opinion, which I've forgotten (my fault, not the estimable Friedman's), but a mention in passing of some news from the poetry world. Computers are now writing poems that pass for poems by people.

I hadn't been aware of this development, but it isn't terribly surprising. Computers have been writing convincing-sounding music for a while now, and chimpanzees, not to mention elephants, have been painting canvasses that aren't just passable but salable, so it only stands to reason that a program can write something indistinguishable from poetry by a human. I'm thinking in particular of the dissociative sort of poetry that inspired the title of the critic Stephen Burt's engaging book about it, *Close Calls with Nonsense*. (Burt emphasises the 'close calls' part; another critic might have proceeded differently.) I'm no programmer, but I don't see why the production of such poetry couldn't be automated: hook a lexicon up to a randomiser and you'd be halfway home. It would be harder to program the writing of a more sensible sort of poetry, though to go by the existence of code that produces decent prose (which tends to make at least a bow to reason), such programming wouldn't seem to be impossible.

But even the cleverest code would have trouble coming up with something like the opening of W. S. Merwin's 'For the Anniversary of My Death':

Every year without knowing it I have passed the day
When the last fires will wave to me

And the silence will set out
Tireless traveler
Like the beam of a lightless star

As hard as it would be for a program to generate the beautiful figures for death in these lines, it would be even harder for a program to generate the premise behind these figures: that 'every year without knowing it' one passes what will be one's death-day. Such a thought only occurs to something mortal, haunted, and subject to inspiration. I'd be the first to tip my hat to a program that answers to this description, but I've yet to run into one.

Degas once told Mallarmé that he was bursting with ideas for poems. Mallarmé's famous response was that poems are made of words, not ideas. One sees his point, but would it be asking too much of a mind to think that a poem could be made of words and ideas alike? I hope not, because many fine poems – Merwin's, for one – are made in this way. And it's good that they are, since a strong idea in a poem, like a great theme in a symphony, may be (as the conceptual germ of Merwin's poem arguably is) its most memorable element.

Mallarmé is hardly the only poet to question the propriety of ideas in poetry. (Maybe the paradigm case of such questioning is Archibald MacLeish's, 'A poem should not mean / but be'.) And yet who's to say that what's most likely in a poem to survive the fraying of one's memory – not to mention the windblown sands of time – wouldn't be an idea? Or that an idea in a poem mightn't turn out to be the most human thing about it?

Letter from Wales

A FEW WEEKS AGO I applauded, at a distance, the launch of a fresh reprint of the first, and best, 1828 edition of *Twm Shon Catti*. Its author, Thomas Jeffery Llewelyn Prichard, would have been delighted: a new edition with sundry minor blemishes in the original, like the eccentric numbering of chapters, removed, and it didn't cost him a penny. The book is edited by Rita Singer in the Llyfrau Cantre'r Gwaelod series (a branch of Celtic Studies Publications, or CSP) dedicated to returning to print Welsh literary classics of the nineteenth century. I doff my cap to it, while Prichard capers.

He would have been less cheerful to receive a charge of plagiarism, from an anonymous critic, who alleges he helped himself to verses that were composed by another, namely Mrs Catherine George Ward. I will admit I had never previously heard of her, and hastened to make her acquaintance. The

Oxford Dictionary of National Biography tells us she was born in 1787, somewhere in Scotland, spent her childhood 'partly in the Isle of Wight' and 'had family connections in Norfolk'. She made a handful of appeals to the Royal Literary Fund to tide her over existential crises, sick children and insolvent husbands dying of TB. The disease may have claimed her, too, for nothing is known of her after 1833. Biographically she is as shadowy a figure as Prichard, or probably more so.

Mrs Ward (Mrs Mason by her second marriage) was a prolific novelist, and for much of her career had a well-known publisher, George Virtue, ready to bring out anything she produced. Several of her books were originally issued in parts, a style of publication that first made Virtue's name. You can find a good sample of her doorstop fictions digitised online. Two I read because they relate to the case, a third, chosen at random, to test whether Jane Austen had anything to fear from this younger contemporary. The short answer is no.

Mrs Ward, unlucky in her husbands and likely driven by the constant threat of poverty, was industrious and possessed astonishing facility. Between 1810 and 1833 she seems to have churned out nineteen novels, most easily exceeding 600 pages. In all circumstances, narrative or descriptive, hyperbole is Mrs Ward's default setting. She attempts wit but is seriously lacking in humour. Irony is unknown to her. In the books I have read her main characters are all titled, 'excessively' handsome or beautiful, 'prodigiously' wealthy and gifted, noble, courageous, sensitive, modest, generous and altruistic. The faults a few may have, due to a quick mind and youthful lack of polite inhibition, they lose at the first serious turn. The conflict in young people between love and duty owed to parents and the magnetic attraction of another is a reiterated theme. They easily betray their true feelings for a blush accompanies any and every emotion.

Women and men are much given to 'colouring deeply'. From time to time, especially when acting or about to act nobly, characters refer to themselves in the third person: 'And when Edwin proves himself unworthy, may he that moment cease to live.' They rarely 'say' anything; even mundane expressions in direct speech are accompanied by, 'he cried' or 'she exclaimed' or even 'ejaculated'. Popular appeal was Mrs Ward's goal and to attain it she created cartoon characters and situations. She is an early nineteenth-century Mills and Boon romancer, love and marriage the fulcrum of action. Thwarted love can lead to sickness and even tubercular death, and tears are shed, copiously, on all sides, but finally romantic love triumphs. Babies are born, without stress, and beautiful, of course. The education of children is entrusted to tutors, male and female, who may be harmlessly eccentric but are devoted to their charges and are likely to get paired off in the knot-tying of the resolution.

This is not to say she never made observations on the social life of the period, but they are rare and lack spirit or spite. Publishers affect to despise authors whose second work cannot be obtained at 'so cheap a price as the first'; women in society disparage 'darkly complexioned' children 'allied to some tawny breed', or any seen to make a successful match ahead of their own; other women, who give up their children to a wet nurse, are derided as 'cruel' and 'unnatural'. Along with the 'penurious and shabby prices of booksellers' that starve authors, breast-feeding was an issue Mrs Ward took very seriously.

Where does Prichard come into this? Mrs Ward's first book was a slim volume of poems, sold by subscription, and most of her novels are liberally sprinkled with poetry. Every chapter has an epigraph, and quite often further lines of verse and even complete poems turn up in the text. Among the acknowledged suppliers of epigraphs are Shakespeare, Campbell, Pope, Burns, Phillips, Goldsmith, Rogers, Moore, Byron, Southey, Scott, Gray and Crabbe. Many more are unattributed, including extracts from early plays. As a young woman, Mrs Ward was an actress (the subscribers' list to *Poems*, 1805, suggests a connection with the Theatre Royal, Edinburgh, though no record of her stage career has emerged) but the lines from, for example Dekker's *Old Fortunatus*, are not quoted from memory, nor do they necessarily indicate familiarity with the play. Rather they are gathered from the selections of poetic and dramatic fragments published in magazines, such as Leigh Hunt's *The Indicator*.

The chosen passages are occasionally abbreviated or otherwise modified. Such is the case with the epigraph to chapter VIII of *The Fisher's Daughter, or the Wanderings of Wolf and the Fortunes of Alfred* (1824), where eight lines are assembled from three separate stanzas of Prichard's 'The Star of Liberty', with his name (misspelled Pritchard) attached. Later in the same chapter the complete poem is presented as the work of the 'young inspired poet' Wolf. In chapter XIV, Wolf's 'tribute to the young sister Anne' is actually Prichard's 'A Quaker Beauty's Likeness'. His authorship is given away by the lines: 'Thy sister-maids my heart admires. / Like Cambrian girls of farthest shires, / Simplicity and truth are theirs, / My countrywomen.' Both substantial borrowings, 104 and 72 lines respectively, vary in numerous minor ways from the texts printed in his *Mariette Mouline, The Death of Glendower and other poems* (1823), which may indicate Mrs Ward's taste in punctuation was less prone to the exclamation mark and dash than Prichard's, or that she had copied from earlier manuscript versions.

The title alone which Mrs Ward chose for her next novel, *The Mysteries of St. Clair, or Mariette Mouline* (1824) inspired the charge of plagiarism. Read on! one might say, for in chapter XXVI 'Mariette Mouline', the title poem of Prichard's book, all 122 lines, is quoted as the poetic account of 'a lonely and unfortunate woman' to Zosinsky, 'the great Tartarian conqueror' who, in his thoughtless youth, had seduced and abandoned her. Inevitably, at the end of the novel they marry. Prichard tells us he borrowed the story from Kotzebue's *Anecdotes, Literary and Philosophical*. As his notes to the poem go on to explain, to avoid confusion with Sterne's 'Maria at Moulines' in *A Sentimental Journey*, he changed the name of the betrayed woman from 'Maria Moulin', as Kotzebue has it, to 'Mariette'. Far from being stolen from Mrs Ward, 'Mariette Mouline' was his invention. The tale is extrinsic to the narrative development of Mrs Ward's book and might have been added to make up the pages of the final 'part' at its initial publication.

That's speculation, of course, but why stop there? Is the description of Wolf in The Fisher's Daughter, with his 'fine intelligent dark piercing eyes', his tall stature and 'great propensity for literature' a portrait of Prichard? Is the concern that lines in 'The Star of Liberty' are 'inflammatory', so that 'it were far better he had not expressed' them, Mrs Ward's concern on behalf of her friend at a time when literary attacks on the establishment could lead to arrest and imprisonment? I have no doubt she and Prichard were friends. They had in common experience on stage and ambition to make a living by the pen and she was a ready customer for Prichard's far bigger collection of poems, *Welsh Minstrelsy*. In the subscribers' list of that book we find '*Warde, Mrs Catherine George, London (6 copies)'. The 'Star' preceding the name denotes an especial closeness; '6 copies' the generosity of her support.

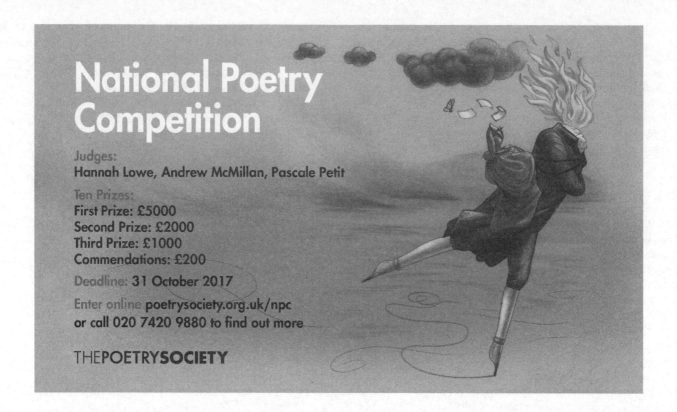

From the Journals of R. F. Langley

THE POET R. F. LANGLEY (1938–2011) was also, privately, a prolific prose writer. Extracts from his journals, which he began in 1969, first appeared in *PN Review* in 2002. The notes to Langley's *Complete Poems*, edited by Jeremy Noel-Tod, cite a number of unpublished journal entries that directly informed the writing of his verse.

25 MARCH 2006

Venice

The Salizada is stone, stone-floored, stone- or stucco-walled, lamplit and empty behind me. Suddenly B. and Eric appear from it, calling me. Eric had passed on one of the vaporettos I had seen, discovered they do not stop at San Samuele at this time of night – a fact I was beginning to deduce after half an hour – and gone on to the Accademia, coming over the bridge there and getting to the flat that way. B. had looked down from our window and seen the shadow of a man in the street, the figure itself hidden below the sill and the balcony and window box of the window below. She heard the rustling of paper, and guessed it was Eric checking his map before ringing – so she called down. So here he is, more or less on time, from Edinburgh via Frankfurt. He had seen me as he passed on the boat, it must have been me... across the water. In my solitude I was noticed. Long journeys had brought us on time together, separate still, not quite meeting yet, one seeing the other but not being sure, me seeing the boat and wondering what it would be like if he were on it and it didn't stop here. Greetings. Embraces. In this stone place, this watery place, this echoing place, this place softly modelled in pale lamplight, nothing less than the Grand Canal, in Venice, as it were emptied, almost, of other people so it becomes a stage for our meeting. A quality stage. A fine doorway topped with a coat of arms and its carved border. Little balconies with balustrades under windows. A campanile over the roofs. A few of the big, high-windowed rooms lit from within, round this small campo. Eric and B. as black silhouettes, striding out together, calling me.

Neither Near Nor Far Away

JUDITH WILLSON

per il mar senz'onde e senza lidi,
le péste né vicine né lontane.
— Giovanni Pascoli, 'Nella nebbia'

You are thinking about hens,
how they bubble like kettles,
how they hitch up their skirts
and scuttle like busy women.

Your grey sisters whisper
you must not be disturbed.
Your good household women.

Hens with their old red eyes,
their sideways calculations.
They do not miss a single grain of maize,
scrabbling like women in the market
who have only one coin left.

How long ago
a circle of girls in the evening, heads bent,
tearing open papery husks, songs
thrown and caught in a ring. The maize
amber, swollen with milk.

How long ago
the night a grey mare trotted home
through the worn-out smell of August roads,
her reins trailing,
a dead man hanging over the saddle.

There was always a secret road to a green wood.
Always fathers and brothers were watching.

*

This is your life without words,
your caterpillar life
that eats at the starry green light
in your mind's tight-folded heart.

Sour kitchen smells, vinegar and lentils,
pig-killing winters, the village blood and dung.
A body hung and emptied like an old coat.
The tongue cut out and salted.

Winter was a room under a low roof
where your mother lay silent,
distinguished in her carved marriage bed,
slowly travelling out of her bones.

Your sisters wore jet beads,
filled your bowl with soup. Yellow pork fat
like the comfort of candles.
Your good grey women.

*

Old men on trams in quiet northern towns
carry boxes of cakes on Sunday mornings.
In the hills, their villages are empty,

streets curl in the sun like cats
round a church and a plane tree,

an alley into someone's courtyard
tangled in ropes and broken crates,
a window to a neighbour's storeroom.
Sacks of chestnuts and lentils for the winter.

A grey mare passed this way on a hot August night.

They knew the man who came home
hung over the saddle like the deer
fathers and brothers would shoot in the woods
where women picked strawberries
and girls walked arm in arm after work.

They knew his neighbour
who has not yet come home.

You buy cakes for your sisters on Sunday mornings,
read Virgil in the evenings. On hot August nights
you sit on your balcony, watch swallows
dart over the square until dark.
Leaves rattle in the fountain's dry basin.

Your father rides his grey mare home
and your mother waits, saying *How late it is,*
I heard the last train pass hours ago.

*

A man leaves and does not return
and nothing changes. Or
a man leaves and does not return
and everything changes.

Hens scratching dust in the maize stubble,
girls idling home from the fields.
Sheep brought down from the hills,
their bulging yellow eyes.
The village locked in its hunger.

All night the dogs bark at something
that leaves its stink in the orchard.
Fathers and brothers will go to the woods.
They know the paths, the trampled grass,
the torn branches.

Old women know how the story is told.
They keep it in a linen bag
filled with lavender and rue.
Never cut bread with a knife.
Drip olive oil into water.
Watch the little planets roll,
grassy gold as lamps in windows.

The shirt she gave him is white.
It hangs on a hedge, arms spread,
heavy with night mist.

*

How long ago
a grey mare and a white road.
A locked room. A story
that always begins in late summer
in ripe maize, the crackle of husks.
Girls' voices sing you through a green wood.
Their feet leave no prints.

And one day the swallows are gone,
the swifts have fallen silent. All summer
they never touched the ground.
A man's face becomes transparent as old linen.

You sit here with your book
in a small resort on a blue October evening,
thinking about hens.
The restless sea gnaws at the harbour,
strings of coloured lights flap in the rising wind.
A boy shuts the café door.

The Lives of Robert Lowell

TONY ROBERTS

'I can't tell you how I dread the future with biographies and Lizzie, to say nothing of Cal,
who will never be even touched with the truth of his own being and nature.'
– Elizabeth Hardwick to Elizabeth Bishop (18 October, 1973)

IN *Reading Chekhov: A Critical Journey* (2001), Janet Malcolm wrote of 'the inescapable triviality of biography', since the artist's doings are 'the mere husk of the kernel of our essential life'. There may be all sorts of things wrong with this, though it also feels true in some way. Nonetheless biography can be a revealing, fascinating and potent force. It can illuminate the work of an artist, affect our perspective on it and, most worryingly, overwhelm what is supposedly its *raison d'être*.

All three outcomes have been the fate – to date – of the biographies and reminiscences of the American poet Robert Lowell (1917–77), once the premier poet in the English speaking world. First came the brilliant but severe *Robert Lowell: A Biography* (1982) by Ian Hamilton, which effectively tarred its subject. Then came Paul Mariani's admiring *Lost Puritan: A Life of Robert Lowell* (1994) – honest and informative, but insufficient to redress the balance. There followed *Collected Poems* (2003), *The Letters of Robert Lowell* (2005) and *Words in Air: The Complete Correspondence Between Elizabeth Bishop and Robert Lowell* (2008), all of which have done something for the reputation, along with a host of other studies and essays over the years, notably by Helen Vendler, Richard Tillinghast, Alan Williamson, Steven Gould Axelrod and William Doreski. There have been romantic memoirs by Kathleen Spivack, one forthcoming by Sandra Hochman and a scandalous outing by Jeffrey Meyers. In short, there is a continuing Lowell industry, though of late more focused on the life than the poetry.

Now we have the much anticipated *Robert Lowell: Setting the River on Fire* by Kay Redfield Jamison, the reviews of which – by Lowell intimates – are startling ('I'm happy that I've lived long enough to read it', Frank Bidart; 'In this astonishingly multidimensional portrait of Robert Lowell, Jamison makes him live and breathe', Jonathan Raban). Jamison, an eminent psychiatrist, makes it clear that hers is not a biography but 'a psychological account of the life and mind of Robert Lowell; it is as well a narrative of the illness that so affected him, manic-depressive illness'.

The photographs on the covers of the three major studies signal their degrees of sympathy. The Hamilton book bore a slightly manic illustration and, in paperback, a photo of an unkempt Lowell, shock of greying hair, eyes averted. The Mariani offered a 'Life' portrait from 1947: the young Lowell as a Hollywood dreamboat. Jamison's biography has a photo by Gisèle Freund of an alert Lowell, wearing jacket and tie on a Parisian terrace in 1963. Hers is the portrait of an intellectual.

Robert Traill Spence Lowell IV – Cal to his friends – had a privileged Bostonian upbringing marred by a difficult home life and a struggle with self-control at school. Unhappy at Harvard, he was taken in by the Fugitive poets of Tennessee, Allen Tate and John Crowe Ransom, following the latter to Kenyon College, Ohio, where he made lifelong friendships, including that with Randall Jarrell. He began writing difficult and powerful poems fuelled by religious imagery and intolerance for the fallen world of New England and Europe. The publication of the Pulitzer Prize-winning *Lord Weary's Castle* in 1946 made his reputation.

Lowell was much honoured in his life, book after book winning awards. He developed wide literary friendships, constantly revised his poems and his style, and was offered prestigious teaching appointments. He also developed a public persona: telling off presidents, opposing the offensive militarism of the Second World War (for which he was imprisoned as a conscientious objector) and marching against the Vietnam War. At that time, he dabbled briefly in politics as an 'aid' to Eugene McCarthy in 1968 and flirted with the Kennedy clan.

Lowell was frequently hospitalised from 1949 onwards with bipolar disorder – the latest victim of an auspicious New England family line – which expressed itself in bouts of intense work, religious zealotry, infidelity, lavish expenditure and destructive behaviour, spiralling into breakdown and guilty depression. Apparently, in the early stages of a manic attack, Lowell was 'seductive, flush with words and ideas and confidence', hardly even recognisably ill. Soon, as he described it to Elizabeth Bishop, 'These things come on with a gruesome, vulgar, blasting surge of "enthusiasm", one becomes a kind of man-aping balloon in a parade – then you subside and eat bitter coffee-grounds of dullness, guilt etc.'

A dramatic, though temporary, conversion to Catholicism accompanied his marriage to the first of three writer wives, Jean Stafford, a marriage productive but destructive. Later his zeal would find expression not in religion but in love affairs. Elizabeth Hardwick, his second wife, was in good part responsible for Lowell surviving the attacks of mania. In contrast he found his third marriage, to Caroline Blackwood, in England, wonderful but eventually intolerable. Lowell finally returned to life with Hardwick, dying in a taxi cab outside their home.

All this is the material for the two biographies and this new study of the life and mind. What is interesting is what is considered, what is omitted, where the interpretative accent lies and, ultimately, how close we come to Malcom's 'husk' and 'kernel'.

Ian Hamilton's authorised biography of Lowell recounts key episodes well and gives lots of mayhem on the way, but is not even understanding enough of the 'mere husk' of the life. It is a portrait of the poet as bad boy. In Jamison's words, 'The Lowell that Hamilton chose to portray is loutish, mad, humorless, a snob, and an overrated poet.' Unsurprisingly, some reviews seized on the image; it made excellent copy. The reader senses from the off that Hamilton does not particularly like his subject. Armed with Lowell's own negative recollections – from prose pieces such as '91 Revere Street' and the letters ('I was so abristle and untamed') – Hamilton warms to his task of presenting an 'ominous nativity'. Lowell's father is 'less than forceful', his mother appalling: 'she would spend whole afternoons waiting for the doorbell to ring so that her servant could announce that she was not at home'.

Enter Lowell, 'utterly enthralled' by the authoritarian ways of a mother he despised. Subjected to the barbarism of private school, he is remembered as 'dark, menacing, belligerent... always ready to take his own unpopularity for granted'. His interest in toy soldiers and military history is seen as grounds for his 'bloodthirstiness'. When Lowell turns to intellectual pursuits Hamilton describes only an 'awesome deliberateness in Lowell's metamorphosis from lout to man of sensibility'. At Harvard he is 'the young malcontent'. The poet's own amusing description of his arrival at the Tates's house in Tennessee is dismissed for the 'sneakily whimsical but condescending tone' that 'was to become familiar to Lowell's Southern friends throughout his later life'. Faced with the paradox of presenting a brutal conscientious objector in later life, Hamilton

decides: 'Most of his childhood heroes had been military heroes, and he had shown himself to have a rare appetite for both tyranny and violence, but he could see little that was splendid in the way modern wars were fought.'

When it comes to the bad behaviour, Hamilton refuses to join the dots. It is as if everything before Lowell's first manic attack is simply brutish behaviour or rebellion. And yet Hamilton knows the plot; he knows what's coming. Even Lowell's fierce, blinkered mother recognises in Lowell's behaviour a 'mental seizure'. Again, after her death, Hamilton writes of 'a new voice to be heard in the letters'. There are, for instance, 'callously brisk accounts of his new financial gains'. Yet this is clearly from an acutely manic letter to Lowell's friend Blair Clark, which his biographer fails to make clear.

Hamilton has no access to Lowell's hospital records and limited sympathy for the mania. He gives, for example, Lowell's lengthy description of a psychotic episode and follows it with the observation that it is 'chillingly consistent with the tone he used to recall childhood misdeeds. There is an amused, tolerant, near embarrassment as Lowell recalls the 'mischief' he has done – in both schoolroom and asylum.' To Hamilton it seems self-indulgent. Jamison, who has access to the records, has the context: 'Tellingly, Lowell does not write about the subject he broached most often with his doctor: his unshakeable fear that he would go mad again.'

Hamilton also fails to pursue the other Lowell. As Hamilton's friend Al Alvarez wrote in his *Observer* review of the biography, it is 'as if the eminently sane man who wrote the poems ceased to exist in his last years. I find this misleading.' According to writer Peter Taylor, Hamilton missed the fact that 'He was a wonderful friend; he could make you feel good about anything [...] He had the most marvelous sense of humor; he was the gentlest person and the most loyal of friends.' Hamilton also fails to explore this tribute of Hardwick's, written at a time when she was most hurt by Lowell's betrayal: 'I have always felt that the joy of his 'normal' periods, the lovely time we had, all I've learned from him, the immeasurable things I've derived from our marriage made up for the bad periods. I consider it all a gain of the most precious kind.'

Where Hamilton scores – aside from his thorough coverage of the public persona – is with the poetry – when he likes it. He cogently explains the evolution of style that produced Lowell's masterpiece, *Life Studies*, in 1959: 'He had become expert at contriving [prose] sentences that could be elevated and yet speakable, and had found a literary voice that could encompass something of his social self [...] The obvious next step for Lowell was to perceive that some, if not all, of these considerable gains could be carried over into poetry [...] The "excitement" of poetry could vitalize and be restrained by the sturdy, detailed worldliness of prose.'

When he does not like Lowell's poetry, as John Carey acknowledged in his review, Hamilton 'quotes damaging criticisms' and 'adds some of his own'. Not infrequently he is flip. After *Lord Weary's Castle* the poet 'now deals not in destruction but in decline, and he no longer pretends that God is on his side'.

So 'For the Union Dead' is 'his first step towards extending the possibilities of his self-centredness: towards treating his own torments as metaphors of public, even global, ills'.

Reviewing the second major biography of Lowell, *Lost Puritan*, his friend Grey Gowrie wrote in the *Daily Telegraph* (11 February 1995) that Paul Mariani 'has a less forensic mind than Hamilton and on occasion writes slackly'. However, he described the portrait that emerged of the poet as being truer than Hamilton's. Unlike his predecessor's biography Paul Mariani's is sympathetic enough – 'tactful' as Richard Wilbur judged; 'poignant' according to David Ignatow – to see his subject at times through his friends' eyes and therefore brings us close to the 'husk' of Lowell's life.

It is certainly a more approving biography. Mariani noted in his preface: 'my admiration for Lowell and his work only increased as I entered more deeply into his life'. After a dubious beginning in which he imaginatively ranges through Lowell's mind in early July 1954, Mariani settles into a detailed narrative, perhaps lacking Hamilton's stylistic flair, but more interested in the man and less dramatic about the drama.

Mariani treats Lowell's early family life with a little more restraint, dwelling on the influence of the maternal grandfather ('the man who had so shaped him and his mother') and Lowell's father and mother ('Charlotte Hideous' Jean Stafford called her). The welcome addition to the life, however, is the detail on Lowell's first marriage, to Stafford. We share more than her colourful personality and the poisonous, witty comments of her letters, as Mariani brings into focus Stafford's influence on early Lowell. He also invests a little more time in describing the young poet's formative time with the Tates, Ransom and Kenyon. He introduces others with walk-on parts, which develop the narrative, such as publisher James Laughlin (of New Directions) and later Philip Levine, who counters the general admiration by offering a negative assessment of Lowell as a self-involved teacher at Iowa.

Mariani is no apologist for Lowell's behaviour. He notes on more than one occasion how Lowell distanced himself from his own occasionally violent domestic acts. Also, while he resists the pressure to be dramatic about Lowell's harrying of his wives, he does not hide his subject's dominating manner or infidelities. Yet he is sympathetic in dealing with the pressures Lowell is under.

Mariani is often interesting on the poetry, on 'Skunk Hour' for instance, 'Lowell's "Dover Beach"'. In 1953, 'He spent all his spare time writing now, telling Tate that it broke "one's heart each time fighting one's verbiage and awkwardness to the real flesh".' He presents the urgency and frustration Lowell experienced in attempting to evolve as a poet. He had to unlearn, as it were, the lessons of Eliot and Tate, the pressure on tradition, the belief in constantly reinvigorating the old metrical forms, to embrace the lived life in his poetry as he began to see William Carlos Williams had done. Lowell is aided in this recognition by his readings with the Beat poets and a new feeling for freer verse. Yet even at his most successful in experimenting with more relaxed rhythms, he acknowledges that he misses 'the carpentry of definite meter'. Then, when he turns to sonnets, he finds, in Mariani's words, 'a way of mixing the instant with the deeper horizons of history, what he called the "flash of haiku to lighten the distant"'. In his last book, *Day by Day*, published weeks before his death, the poet had turned again, this time solely to free verse.

Mariani is also effective at presenting Lowell's meditations on his art and its accomplishment, by mining the letters and late poems. Lowell comes to think of the 'seedy grandiloquence of *Notebook*'. Reading through his *Selected Poems*, he sees his old preoccupations treated in too similar a way ('half-amused to think he could ever have thought of himself "as a tireless surpriser"'). He wonders what he is doing in England, why a true artist would want to leave his familiar landscape, 'and while his method was "formidable enough to turn out new poems", it was not so easy – or even possible – to turn out new subjects'. Finally, though, Lowell confessed to Frank Bidart, poet and executor, 'that he didn't know what the value of his work would finally be', but he felt he had 'somehow "changed the game"'.

Kay Redfield Jamison's *Robert Lowell: Setting the River On Fire* is ambitious: 'I am interested in who Robert Lowell was, how he came to be the man and poet he was, and why his poetry matters; in what we can learn from his work about the ambition of art, the necessity for art [...] the strands that link madness to action and imagination [...] I am particularly interested in why character [...] matters so deeply in understanding both art and mental illness.' In a way the book is a gift to psychiatry, for Lowell is the ultimate public case study, a subject so highly documented by himself and his friends in poems, essays, letters, remembered conversations and memoirs: 'Hardwick and Lowell left a written legacy of madness, imagination, and determination that is unmatched.' Jamison's starting point, then, is the documentation, 'the lighted way into it'.

Immediately the reader has the illusory feeling that the subject's intimates had held back until now, waiting for a writer like this. For instance, in two early pages Jamison gives testimony to Lowell's unique stimulating brilliance from Alan Brownjohn, Helen Vendler and Esther Brooks (a former ballerina, who gave an acute portrait in the essay 'Cal Remembered'). In Hamilton's biography we find the three also there, but late in the book and commenting on Lowell's behaviour. Similarly, if we turn to the indices of the three biographies we find entries in the Jamison for 'friendships' and 'generosity and kindness'. Hamilton has no such headings. Mariani has 'friendships'. Not damning of course but perhaps a small indicator of the slant of the books.

Jamison begins by restoring Lowell to his ancestors, beginning with Harriet Brackett Spence Lowell, the poet's great-great-grandmother who died insane, and to the New England literary tradition to which he was heir. Generally, there is a relative dearth of action, a focus on character more than incident. Much of the detail of conventional biography is missing, as are certain episodes: details of his student years in the South; a blow-by-blow of the first marriage; the courtship of Elizabeth Hardwick. There is little of Lowell's political activities, of his relationship with other poets, and little on his lovers or students – no Plath, for instance. This should not work to the book's advantage but it does, raising a mirror to the mental life actually more than to the personality.

The mania is central, as is explaining what Lowell's bipolar disorder actually means and meant to him. Particularly relevant is this description of symptoms, from the diagnostic criteria for mania and depression (2013): 'Excessive involvement in activities that have a high potential for painful consequences (e.g. engaging in unrestrained buying sprees, sexual indiscretions, or foolish business investments).' Lowell's reputation has been hurt by his infidelities, his repeated attempts to leave Hardwick for younger women ('All life's grandeur / is something with a girl in summer'). Yet his wife, though repeatedly heartbroken by them, saw Lowell's betrayals during illness as an attempt to begin a new, healthier life, a 'kind of flight' in her words. The identification with men of violence – another blow to Lowell's reputation – becomes, as Jamison explains, something Lowell shared with 'many patients with manic delusions'. To read a Lowell biography without this understanding is to dismiss his behaviour as typical Lowell high-handedness.

What Jamison achieves is to make the life a whole, to make it meaningful and to see its essential courage. 'Lowell came back from madness time and again, reentered the fray, and kept intact his friendships. He kept his wit and his capacity for love.' The manic episodes are no longer only tragic breaks in the living and writing routine but the accelerating rhythm that also produced the work: 'Mania took his poetry where it would not have gone'. In the dry periods 'it disturbed the embers and breathed back the life into his poetry'. To Jonathan Raban Lowell once reported, 'I write in mania and revise in depression.' If he could only control the mania, he would have accepted it, cost and all. It could not produce great poetry but it could get the motor running. Whether, in fact, the early poetry suffered from the manic flights and the later poetry suffered from the lithium remains contestable.

Jamison filters Lowell's unpleasant behaviour – the broken confidences, the betrayals, the violence – through his mania. In so doing she gets closer to the genius and courage and this, presumably, is what his intimates so admire about the book: 'Few can prevail against mental illness as severe as Lowell's; still less can they re-enter the mix of life, as he did time after time.' She invokes comparisons with explorers (Scott) and poet-warriors (Sassoon). Her conclusion is that 'Robert Lowell knew civic valor. Sixteen times and more he had been down on his knees in madness, he said. Sixteen times and more he had gotten up. He had gone back to his work, entered back into life. He had faced down uncertainty and madness.'

What is the dark side of the man, his illness aside? Jamison does not allow, as Hamilton did, for 'an element of simple mischief, of sly, childishly perverse outrageousness' in his breakdowns. The furthest she will go is to make comment on 'the relentless mind' and 'vaulting ambition' (I am reminded of a comment by Lincoln's law partner: 'His ambition was a little engine that knew no rest'). It is as if Lowell's mania is enough for the reader to deal with and the wonderful qualities of the man must be ranged against it. This is Jamison's way. Although she cautions her readers at the outset that no one can more than partly understand the mind of another, she comes enviably close to illuminating moments of what Janet Malcolm referred to at the outset as her subject's 'essential life'.

In the 6 January edition of the *TLS* this year, the 'NB' column had this to say of Lowell in its anniversaries: 'In the 1960s and '70s, Lowell was No. 1... Nowadays he scarcely figures in the Top Twenty. His early formal verse is too highly wrought for modern taste, and his late work too diffuse.' In my view there are no American poems of the last fifty years that stand with 'The Quaker Graveyard in Nantucket', 'Waking Early Sunday Morning' or 'For the Union Dead' as public poems, or 'Man and Wife', 'The Old Flame', or 'Home after Three Months Away' as painful, personal testimonies. One can argue that all day, but not about the bankability of a dramatic life:

I have sat and listened to too many
words of the collaborating muse,
and plotted perhaps too freely with my life,
not avoiding injury to others,
not avoiding injury to myself –
to ask compassion

('Dolphin')

Robert Lowell has received more 'compassion' than he might have felt he earned. It is time to do justice to his poetry again. For us, at least, the 'essential self' is there.

At the Brasserie Lipp

MICHAEL EDWARDS

1

Sitting in Lipp's with this in-
fernal ticking in the ink I find myself
remembering the quiet of Manhattan, the low-slung
crooning cabs with Rolls-Royce engines
shushing the sidewalk buzz, gliding
on soft rubbers along the deep pile
of roadway like butlers in Wodehouse;
and did they really smell
so sweet? Was that Persian air
odours from the bay or whiffs of perfumed petrol?

*

In the church over there, which gave its name
to a whole way of life, and now squats
on a square devoted to the stars of the fifties,
I heard all those years ago the handsome voice
of Pierre Emmanuel. Did I understand
the poems, with my Cambridge French? Were there truly
so many women, agog like Philaminte?
Poetry as fiery reason, he wrote, a mind
that has the good sense of a body wholly
in touch with the world and ready for the exact
exacting flames of the candid, the white-
hot depths. And then
the volume from the *TLS* with his signature
shaking in the corner like an invalid
not long before dying, which by then had occurred.

*

A waiter, distrait, picks the wax from his ear.
The cars, with not a single Simca, go flying past,
honking like geese. I see
in the coffee grouts two boys on an empty road,
swinging their heels against a wall, waiting for the rare
prize of a motor-car, the brilliant
Triumph Gloria, swift-footed Lagonda,
ponderous Standard Vanguard,
to approach down the long perspectives
and enter their little books.

2

A hard rain splashes on the uneven centuries.
We were lucky whose childhood survived
the Second World War, though that is neither
here nor there when I recall the condemned
and crazy tenements down in the *treizième*
where painters of exotic speech perched in eyries
linked by filigree flights of stairs
and stop-gap corridors. They were the elders,
moiling all hours in this provisional world,
each in his cell, to prize
open the cryptogram, from zenith to abyss,
or conjure dazzling elsewheres with Prussian red
and yellow viridian. I felt foreign,
listening open-eyed as the talk passed round
with the budget cocoa, a heady brew.

*

That baby with the candid eyes squeezed by the sun
is probably the *me* the gods prefer
or dislike the least. I deal him
on the table, face up, a winner.
Installed on my mother's early-Norman shoulder,
he stares me out, smiling the way they do,
still-born in the country beyond recall,
on a shiny surface retruding memory.
Dammit, he's the me I prefer, touching her hair,
a chubby fellow, yet the little blighter,
innocuous in Shanklin in the summer of '39
and placed mostly naked on a Channel beach,
lifted his hands and feet promptly from the good sand
and registered dislike, so I was told.

*

Coffee on the Piazza Navona had followed
a station in Keats House, not that he ever
had one. The police
were busy already, stripping the walls,
burning the furniture, cursing their luck,
hurriedly fumigating the meagre room
of the little pig-sick foreigner, pains
his breathless body no longer needed. Beneath
a small pyramid he was being lowered
into the pasture, among the sheep and the goats.
With crowds in the circus scenting spring
and gushing waters plashing on marble basins
in the naked Roman light, one can mourn.

3

At Hastings, now, did we lose or win?
The English, underdogs then and *sympathiques*,
had slogged all down England from Stamford Bridge
(no, not from Chelsea; it's in the North)
and huddled, in the shield-ring, on a hill
by the hoar apple tree near Andredsweald.
You know the story: the dogged English
stood their ground, killing continued all day, until
the Normans made as if to make for their boats,
the cloth-capped English scampered after,
and were considerably hurt when the Normans turned
    and charged.
The natives took a drubbing, were plucked, and that was
one in the eye for English intelligence. One owes
allegiance to Harold as the rightful king
and thanks to William for most of history
and for having become, after so many stubborn Springs
and implacable Autumns, one of us.
As the sun hovers behind banking clouds,
Harold kneels among the tourists in the Waltham ruins.

*

I can imagine it, the Wehrmacht vaunting
in well-drilled high-kicking chorus lines
out there, along the stunned half-empty boulevard.
I can see the iron green that clads them
in the colours of myth and the Teutonic fir-forest,
and the forties hair-dos of the girls that serve them

from behind bars in look-alike restaurants
in a thousand films; and I know
the decency of the two German lads
watching from a bridge as they smoked my father-in-law,
and his, caching arms in the wine-dark earth,
and walking away. England occupied,
insularity breached, one cannot picture.
But then, we won the war,
or we outlived it, as the man said,
through being entirely incapable of imagining
Hitler at Lords.

*

Whether the din that stunned the air
above a cornfield in the place of larks
was a demon patrol of Halifax or Lancaster,
the trace of that passing wonder in a six-year-old
survives in the warren of memory. Exning.
In the East, beyond Tashkent, and Samarkand.
Such a brief
translation to paradise (the scented orchard,
the open skies, the room, the conviction
of being elsewhere) from the thirties estate
to which the child Sigismund usually belonged
visited my dreams for decades as a rare
vision. Though even the later
mile-high insect drone of perfectly civil
airliners traversing the garden heights
of our little house on the Heathrow flight-path
returns as the proper sound of gold-green summer.

4

Sitting here sipping at life it is easy
to float light-minded on the wavelets of now.
I remember, however, the terra firma
of the real world, which included, among other
things I might withdraw from the long and musty
sock of memory, debutantes and haystacks
coming out in their season, not that I made
much contact with either. Where are they now
(I mean it: where are they now?)
that time has pulled the staircase from under the ones
and parcels the others in glossy bin-liners?
After thirty, the real is history.
I think with bewildered affection of those
elders who passed their musing youth
wearing Oxford bags and surfing the crystal-set.

*

Puzzling over Wordsworth, I wonder how
he thought that he had seen the world's glory
vanish with childhood. Had he really
romped in Eden, or did he half-
create that memory in the murk of adolescence,
when he discovered the time of spots?
What I recall is a deal of wailing,
and gnashing of teeth, and of having been
a tyke of the first water. And yet
Vaughan, and his 'angel infancy'. Is it
a recurring dream, beamed from beyond
memory, or (grandfather Wordsworth,
I speak as a fool) a being unable
to be there for the future's brief and furtive
advents in corners caught unawares
by vivid, occasional, new-earthly light?

*

A world in my hand in the dark bedroom,
the glowing orange from the Christmas stocking
I see it now, was a toy Paradise,
a wonder to be remembered, and laid aside.
The sunlight accumulates in high windows
above the agreeable city din,
as once the falling sunlight caught
haphazard, naturally, in the higher branches
of ash, and fir, and pine, like thrown
fires from the end of time, burning the unharmed
and chosen trees. The conflagration
insisted in the green and usual leaves,
consuming attention. I stood in the shadows
and swore with happiness, and watched like a quiet
maniac as the embers slowly faded,
and the bats burgeoned from the neighbouring barns.

5

Astaires curvetting through the evening throng,
bearing their trays like the Statue of Liberty
(with a glimpse of tango as they pass each other),
the domino waiters correct with each
shimmy of the hips and inerrant footwork
the rolling of the waves, as if the brasserie
were afloat, or all of us actors in
the restaurant scene of a thirties motion
picture during the long days
of crossing the Atlantic. All of us were sick
on the Channel ferry with the 2CV suspension
and poor whaleroad-holding in the heaving straits,
until the white-uniformed and diocalm voice
of the Captain assured us all would be well
soon, as we passed 'under the lee of England'.
He was right, the unknown formula worked,
I saw the island and the island centuries
lean over the tiny boat to protect it.

*

Old swords, danged and kerfed,
unsmeared of blood in the slow-breathing
after-battles, these, heavy with age,
wieldy with use and cunning knowledge,
gleamed in the minds of the earliest English
as most of worth. Likewise words,
heard through mists on the open furze,
in the depths of shadowed woods, their warm
thunder rising from the dark body
to roll in the deliberately moving mouth
and part the double brattice of the teeth.
Old words in the ear, soundings of an earlier
speech and settlement in the world's things,
impress the here, the now. I find harbour,
a place for the soul, in seaboard, wharf and mooring.

*

It was a smooth though hardly adroit
Ambassador I drove down the Essex by-ways
and down through the flimsy, unresisting
cells of the centuries to the log church
Saxon adzes had cleft and pitched
in the thick of the wood as the wood's nub:
a house of trees to put their faith in.
Not the stare of a screech-owl but a rip of skin

from an icy Viking nailed to the door
greets, at the timber threshold, and outfaces
uncomprehending questions. Within,
my heart sank, gladly, in the undertow
of the old speech, as the ear's mind
heard in our many, unhurried steps
the naming and wedding tongue of the earth-bound,
sky-bound folk, speaking in ours.
'Floor', 'roof', 'opening', 'rightness', 'depth',
remind me of Greensted, a barn for words.
I stir the wood-ash in the cooling hearth
(here, in the champagne light of Paris)
and find the red fire, living still.

6

My answer to the eternal question is
in the kitchen of a house in Orsay to the south of Paris
(a town where Péguy had been and Mosley was),
at breakfast, I believe, it could have been lunch,
I think it was breakfast, we too were stunned.
And a year later it was Eliot's turn,
in the same small kitchen with the radio on,
the first of so many (radios, I mean,
though deaths as well). I'd always supposed
we'd meet, he'd talk, he'd like my poems,
and be the presence of the barbarous, uncanny
language that had entered and coolly opened
a mind unforewarned of such edges of being.
In the world that whirled indeed the real
was suddenly sly, indifferent, different,
and the work stepped back into the pages of history.

*

Drumming and clicking on the marble top
(tentative morse to any passing muse)
recalls the Eroica – the variations – the lucky
thirteenth and that sudden, stricken hand
falling with rhythmic jerks on the clinking
appoggiaturas, then skeltering by fits
down down the keyboard in zany close-up,
and under the soft round hat, Chico's grin.
Travelling the innerscapes of sound, Beethoven,
did you cross the frontier towards what may be
sidereal calms, or tundra with crystal cities
(strains of silence straining to be heard),
by clowning, cutting up ugly, tumbling
scherzando through disgrace notes into the unknown?

*

One can picture him walking by the water-furlongs,
conversing in the damp streets with civil neighbours,
examining with Hall the store of simples,
or making for London, his horse ambling
under him, through acres of rye, but not
not writing. The very idea! The mind
deserts one at his retiring, dismissing his genie,
at the cool detachment of the gentleman of Stratford.
We have
so much to learn from the man's indifference,
from playscripts in neglected corners of the playhouse,
from his knowledge of immortality, that it is nothing
on earth, from his sober practice of silence,
beyond poetry, his final period.

Did Racine discern the lacing of sweat
on the horse's neck, or hear the harness
creak and abrade, or feel the jar
of each hoof meeting the road as if
along his own four legs, while he galloped
ahead of the others to get the best room?
Now, as a sunburst hazes the window
and slopped wine drips from a neighbouring table,
a housefly whispers in my English ear
that it takes as much courage, when the moment comes,
energy and cunning, to forget all that
as to recall it, and make it matter.

*

Of being elsewhere in the one world,
as the same sun sheds an unfamiliar light,
or the mind journeys with the journeying moon,
I sing, sitting here, and remembering Exning.
We stepped from the train into fields of wheat,
into earthy, shoulder-deep, country lanes,
for the wide-eyed kid a vertiginous pastoral,
a paradise heightened by the passing warplanes'
jocund din. In a strange house,
a stranger to himself, he tasted the different
plums, marrows, radishes, he climbed
into the guardian thick of unknown trees,
and ran through the air
sparkling with the effusion of privet and honeysuckle.
That leap from danger (while the V2s crouched)
to another universe bordering Newmarket
returns unfelt, unthought of, whenever
I see things with another's eyes, moonshadows
people with ourselves a sleeping courtyard,
or a building in a shining window discards its usual look
and the sun sheds its familiar light.

*

By the village pond we encountered a black
Canadian pilot. A neat man,
I seem to remember, gentle of speech.
Back indoors, the boy in his book,
my mother was doomed for having been seen
talking to a darky. Though this was Methodism,
there was madness in it; yet who can judge
the errors of that innocent, guilty time?
Another day we rose as one and stepped
silent from the room, the black lid
having closed on the upright as the offended air
stiffened at the breathtaking title of the song
I'd suggested we join in among the hymns
we'd forgathered to intone in the Sunday parlour.
I was in disgrace, though ignorant of grace,
and pored in my mind over the marvellous lady
whose awaited coming would be round the mountains
when she came, whose pink pyjamas
regardless of weather, would emblazon the day,
whose wild, spectacular being was as more
than real as the manners of a coloured airman.

I recall my mother's name as a maiden
mostly for distant voices on the phone
checking for security. Dalliston. It's rare.
A variant of Dallinson, more audibly Englished.
A William D. came with the Conqueror,
or was here for Domesday, having left
lacy Alençon with a view to plunder
(it takes all sorts). 'Norman blood'?
Thinned for centuries by Anglian peasants
and over the border in Cambridgeshire,
neglected, unrecognised, voiceless, but then
why else this ludic and unseemly yen
for a foreign tongue, to hear it in the murmurs
of a known, unfamiliar world, and in
that friendly other who likes to take over,
moved by some blind, stubborn
stubborn gene
to travel the sounds of a kind of innocence?

*

The door swings to with a recurring *brlnk*.
A dog and a girl trot by on the trottoir.
Le Monde on a nearby table folds
a world of noise in a semblance of peace.
The cars prolong their mathematics, *et là-haut*
cette barbe à papa céleste qui s'effiloche.

(The gusts of wind on the Brighton front,
the eye-watering sun, the strangeness of adults.)
What do they know, these amiable aliens,
that they speak their minds, they pluck their words
from the world's tree regardless of Saussure,
and hear them glittering among the spoons, the
    glasses?
Dumb with amazement, I watch a fictive *neige*
fall on the dreamy outside, its coldness quite
close to the baffled silence of snow.

*

At Agincourt, the Duke of Alençon,
breached by a thrust quite possibly Norman,
fell supine on France, and in the clouding light
dipped his fingers in his guts and wrote
the sign of the bloody cross on his breast.
Did he? Did I make it up? Does it matter?
Poetry is a foreign language, way
down inside one, guilty as hell
like everything else, yet cannily innocent,
in league with things to say them as they are
or as they become in the resounding light.
The church over there sticks out like a sore thumb,
trees walk down the boulevard in search of the forest,
it would be fitting if the broken body
like the wounded soul bore the mark of pardon.

'In the Province of Demons'

DAVID HERMAN

Andrzej Franaszek, *Miłosz: A Biography* (Harvard University Press), 544pp, £30

I MET CZESŁAW MIŁOSZ IN 1991 when Michael Ignatieff and I went to produce a programme about him for BBC Two. Miłosz was already eighty. His years in exile were nearly over. The Berlin Wall had fallen in 1989 and Miłosz had returned to Poland a hero. A few months before we filmed our interview with him, Lithuania had just emerged from the deep freeze of the Cold War. Miłosz had gone back to the country he had grown up in for the first time since 1939. In a later interview in *Paris Review* he said, 'I was made an honorary citizen and attended a mass in the wooden church where I was baptized. But many villages have disappeared. I have to presume enormous numbers of their inhabitants were deported to Siberia [...] I visited the place where I was born, but there was no house, only the bare remnants of a park, and the river is polluted.'

This brief passage is deceptive. Some of these images, which seem casual, do a lot of work. 'The wooden church where I was baptized', for example. Miłosz was a lifelong Catholic. 'If I were asked to say where my poetry comes from,' he once said, 'I would say that its roots are in my childhood. In Christmas carols, in the liturgy of Marian and vesper offices, and in the Bible.' One of his great

Holocaust poems is called, 'A Poor Christian Looks at the Ghetto'. He wasn't just baptised, he was baptised 'in a wooden church', an image of powerful simplicity.

Then there are the 'enormous numbers [...] deported to Siberia'. Miłosz was one of the great poets of witness of the twentieth century. He was a child in Russia during the Revolution. He spent much of the Second World War in Warsaw, where he saw at first-hand what was done to the Jews and wrote some of the great poems about the Holocaust. On 1 August 1944, the day the Warsaw Uprising began, he and his wife were caught in gunfire on their way to a friend's apartment. Al Alvarez described the scene in an article in *The New York Review of Books*:

Face down for hours in a potato field, with machine-gun bullets ripping over his head, Miłosz refused to let go of the book he was carrying. ... The book was *The Collected Poems of T. S. Eliot* in the Faber & Faber edition. All in all, it was a very Polish situation: bullets and modernism, the polyglot in the potato field, ashes and diamonds.

After the war, Miłosz quickly realised what was happening to writers and intellectuals in Poland as the Communists took over. The lies, betrayals and deception. How many of his generation embraced their oppressors to save their lives, to climb the ladder, to get a better apartment. And those were the lucky ones who weren't tortured, made unemployable or deported to the Gulag. What is extraordinary is that from across the Atlantic, where he was working in the Polish embassy, he somehow learned everything there was to know about what it was like to live under Soviet Communism. He defected in 1951 and in 1953 published *The Captive Mind*, which together with *1984* and *Darkness at Noon*, is one of the classic texts of the Cold War. It was an astonishing evocation of the compromises forced on writers and intellectuals in eastern Europe. He understood what only those who saw it close up could imagine, how many are prepared to make a pact with the devil. 'Terror,' he wrote, 'is not, as Western intellectuals imagine, monumental; it is abject, it has a furtive glance.'

The third telling image in that short passage about his return to Lithuania is the polluted river. Miłosz spent most of his life in cities. In Wilno (or Vilnius) and Warsaw, in New York, Washington and Paris, when serving the Polish government, in exile in Paris and San Francisco, and in Krakow where he moved after the fall of Communism and where he finally died in 2004. Yet one of the formative times was a brief moment in his childhood in rural Lithuania. 'The Lithuania of my youth is for me very much alive,' he told an interviewer from *La Stampa* in 1986, 'because the forests, the valleys and the rivers which I saw in my childhood possess for me a strong evocative force'.

Catholicism, history, nature. They run through this short quotation from *The Paris Review*, as they weaved through his life and his poetry. When I met him in 1991 and looked into those extraordinary unblinking eyes, I didn't realise how little I knew of what those eyes had seen.

Now at last we have a biography of Miłosz. At five hundred pages, it is half the length of the huge Polish original, published in 2011, but it has a new introduction by the translators, Aleksandra and Michael Parker, along with maps, photographs and a very useful chronology. The author, Andrzej Franaszek, teaches Polish Literature at Krakow's Pedagogical University and has written two other books, not yet translated, *Dark Source: The Work of Zbigniew Herbert* (2008) and *Pass the Hell: 44 Essays on Literature and the Adventures of the Soul* (Krakow, 2010).

Franaszek provides an admirably clear account of Miłosz's long and troubled life. He slices the cake well, giving due attention to the central chapters of Miłosz's life. He does a good job of balancing the poet's personal life, the historical context and his poetry. His writing is free of jargon and there are many details which are new and illuminating. My only serious criticism is that he is less familiar with the secondary literature in English than one might expect from the author of such a monumental biography. On the other hand, few English-speaking readers will be familiar with the Polish primary and secondary sources that he quotes.

Above all, Franaszek has a good grasp of Polish history and its literary world over more than seventy years and does an excellent job of bringing it to life. In a fascinating essay about Miłosz in *The Three-penny Review* in 2008, the poet and translator Adam Zagajewski wrote:

He belonged to a chapter of the history of Polish literature that seemed to be, seen from the landscape of my youth, as remote as the Middle Ages. He was a part of the last generation that had been born into the world of the impoverished gentry (impoverished but still very much defining themselves as gentry): he grew up in a small manor house in the Lithuanian countryside where woods, streams, and water snakes were as evident as streetcars and apartment houses in the modest, industrial city of my childhood. His Poland was so totally different from mine – it had its wings spread to the East. When he was born in 1911 he was a subject of the Russian Tsar; everything Russian, including the language which he knew so well, was familiar to him (though, as his readers well know, he was also very critical of many things Russian). I was born into a Poland that had changed its shape; like a sleeper who turns from one side to another, my country spread its arms toward the West – of course only physically, because politically it was incorporated into the Eastern bloc.

Zagajewski makes an important point. There used to be a plaque outside the Warsaw Opera House which said you are now at the centre of Europe. Even if we are prepared to think of Warsaw and Krakow as part of central Europe, the world Miłosz grew up in – Russia during the First World War, the Lithuanian countryside, Vilnius/Wilno – is in the east. He read Latin and translated T. S. Eliot, but he grew up on the periphery of Europe, over a thousand kilometres from Prague, closer to St Petersburg than Vienna. When France fell, Arthur Koestler headed for Paris. When Poland fell, Miłosz escaped to Romania.

Miłosz was born in central Lithuania in 1911. His childhood was itinerant, his family moving between Russia, where his father served as an engineer during the First World War, Lithuania and Poland. Or, more precisely, Vilnius where they lived for much of this time, moved between Lithuania and Poland. Miłosz was part of that extraordinary generation of east Europeans who spent their lives on the move, while borders moved around him. Born in Lithuania, he spoke no Lithuanian. Poland's great modern poet, he spent most of his adult life outside Poland, in exile. Almost a decade in Paris. More than thirty years in America. 'Language,' he said, 'is the only homeland.'

Wilno (Vilnius to Lithuanians) was the still point in Miłosz's turning world. His family settled there in 1921. It's where Miłosz went to school (1921–29), then to university (1929–34). At school, he said later, 'I was shaped by seven years of Latin and by exercises in translating Latin poetry in class'. As a student he published his first poems and helped found an avant-garde literary group, Zagary. Their politics were left wing, their poetry experimental, part of what was later called the Catastrophist School. In an essay, 'Appreciating Miłosz', published in *Encounter* in the 1980s, the Polish émigré Leo Labedz wrote about what happened to the group:

One was executed during the Occupation by the Polish Underground for helping the Soviet secret police. Two were killed by the Russians in Katyn in 1940. Two others became very prominent figures in Communist Poland after the War.

After graduating from university, Miłosz worked mainly for Polish Radio, first in Wilno, then in Warsaw. After the outbreak of war he fled to Romania, then returned to Wilno. In 1940, the Red Army marched in. 'And then I saw the devil doing his work', he later told his class of Berkeley undergraduates. After ten months, and having covered thousands of miles, he returned to Warsaw to rejoin his girlfriend (later his first wife), Janina (Janka) Cekalska. He spent most of the Second World War in Warsaw, attending lectures and writing poetry. With his brother he helped rescue several Jews, helping them find shelter. For these efforts, Miłosz received the medal of the Righteous Among the Nations in Yad Vashem in 1989.

He continued to write poetry, including 'A Poor Christian Looks at the Ghetto' and 'Campo de Fiori', two outstanding poems about the fate of the Jews in Poland and the observing gaze of the gentile. 'In the spring of 1943,' he wrote after the war, 'on a beautiful quiet night, a country night in the outskirts of Warsaw, standing on the balcony, we could hear screaming from the ghetto...' At the heart of these poems is the relationship between the witness who survives and the object of his gaze who doesn't. 'But that day I thought only / of the loneliness of the dying.' In the words of Joseph Brodsky, a fellow Nobel Prize-winning poet, 'Out of the scattered ashes emerged poetry which did not so much sing of outrage and grief as whisper of the guilt of the survivor.'

In a later interview, Miłosz said of his writing during this period, 'I was uneasy as a poet, because I had come to understand that poetry could not depict the world as it was – the formal conventions were wrong. So I searched for something different. But at the same time, I wrote a long work consisting of short poems, entitled *The World (A Naive Poem)*, a sequence – though I was not aware of it at the time – like Blake's *Songs of Innocence*. I considered the world so horrible that these childish poems were answers – the world as it should be, not as it was. Written in view of what was happening, *The World* was a profoundly ironic poem.'

After the Second World War, Miłosz and his wife moved to the US. He had a job with the Polish diplomatic service. He later recalled a friend telling him, 'Have it if you want it. But remember, you are signing a pact with devil'. In 1950 he was transferred to the embassy in Paris. He was already an object of suspicion and at one point he had his passport confiscated. Back in Paris, he defected in 1951 and in 1953 published *The Captive Mind*, one of the classic anti-Communist texts of the Cold War. It was an astonishing evocation of the compromises forced on writers and intellectuals in eastern Europe, how so many ended up betraying their ideals and embracing Stalinist oppression.

Miłosz spent the next decade in Paris as a freelance writer, attacked by Polish emigres for taking so long to break with the Communist regime and by French Communists for betraying the Left. Pablo Neruda denounced him as 'The Man Who Ran Away'. 'At that time,' Miłosz said later, 'French intellectuals were completely in love with Communism and Stalin. Anyone who was dissatisfied and who came from the East like myself was considered a madman or an agent of America... At that time the political climate of Europe was dismal; millions of people were in gulags; their suffering contaminated the aura, the air of Europe. I knew what was going on. The West had to wait for Solzhenitsyn to write *The Gulag Archipelago* to learn about it.'

This is the most original part of Franaszek's book, revealing how isolated Miłosz was and how he was driven to depression, close to suicide. 'For me it was reaching rock bottom.' He was in exile, vilified, cut off from his wife and young sons, safe but far away across the Atlantic. During these years, only Camus and a few Polish literary figures stood by him. Above all, he received support from *Kultura*, the best Polish émigré monthly, published in Maisons-Laffitte, that had published his writings from the outset. But there were slim pickings. In 1953, one thousand copies of *Daylight*, a poetry collection, were published. Four years later, 320 remained unsold. Even *The Captive Mind* sold barely 1,700 copies in four years. It took two years for *The Issa Valley* (six hundred copies) to sell out.

In 1960 Miłosz was invited to teach Polish and Russian Literature at Berkeley. He spent more than thirty years in California. At first, he was barely known outside a small circle of students and translators. 'I was completely unknown to almost all my colleagues at Berkeley [...] I was an obscure professor in an obscure department.'

Above all, it was a different world. 'Like one of Dostoyevsky's characters,' writes Franaszek, 'he felt deracinated, transplanted into a civilization where normality meant listening to The Rolling Stones, smoking marijuana, being preoccupied with social revolution and protests against the war in Vietnam. Robert Hass, the poet, recalled a friend of his saying that when she went to the [Miłosz] house on Grizzly Peak [...] she felt as if vibrant, brightly coloured California had simply vanished and that she had suddenly stepped into the interior of a European art-house movie, shot in a grim, dim light.'

The great turning-point came in the late 1970s and '80s. Miłosz was awarded a number of literary prizes. In 1978 Joseph Brodsky presented Miłosz with the Neustadt International Prize for Literature. It was worth $212,000 but Brodsky's words were more important: 'I have no hesitation whatsoever in stating that Czeslaw Miłosz is one of the greatest poets of our time, perhaps the greatest.' Then in 1980 Miłosz was awarded the Nobel Prize. In Poland, a government-authorised edition of Miłosz's poems was issued and sold 200,000 copies. In the United States his poems were widely translated, and from 1983 were published regularly in *The New Yorker*. He was invited to give the Norton lectures at Harvard (published as *The Witness of Poetry*, 1983). He made important friendships with poets like Seamus Heaney and Brodsky, like himself poets from the outer edges of Europe. Crucially, Central Europe emerged from the Cold War. In 1984 Milan Kundera wrote his seminal essay, 'The Tragedy of Central Europe', reminding western readers that the great literary centres of Prague, Budapest and Poland were closer to Vienna and Berlin than to Moscow. Above all, Poland suddenly appeared centre stage. There was a Polish Pope, Solidarity was founded and

Soviet Communism fell. 'A portrait of the Pope was displayed in his house in Berkeley,' writes Franaszek, 'alongside one taken with the poet himself.' When a monument was built in Gdańsk to commemorate the shipyard workers killed by the Polish security police, lines from a verse by Miłosz were engraved on it:

You who wronged a simple man
Bursting into laughter at the crime...
You can kill one, but another is born,
The words are written down, the deed, the date.

Miłosz returned to Poland as a national hero. For some time, he said, he kept a badge he had been given which depicted 'four sacred symbols for Poland; a bishop's mitre, which represented Cardinal Wyszynski; keys, the Pope; electric tools, Walesa; and a book, Miłosz'. He settled in Cracow in 1993 for the last ten years of his life. When he died in 2004 among the ten thousand who came to say farewell in person were Lech Walesa and Adam Michnik; the film director, Andrzej Wajda and fellow poets Wislawa Szymborska and Seamus Heaney.

Franaszek captures this life in all its complexity and darkness. Miłosz was a modern Job, tried by personal sadness and historical catastrophe. He lived in exile for forty years. His younger son endured a long period of severe mental illness. His first wife suffered from motor neurone disease for the last ten years of her life. Miłosz outlived her and his second wife, Carol, his brother and many of his oldest friends.

We can perhaps divide Miłosz's life and writing into three parts. In the 1940s and '50s he was preoccupied with politics, history and philosophy. Over the next twenty years, he was more drawn to theology, religion and God. The morning Miłosz was awarded the Nobel Prize, a friend got a call from the *New York Times*:

'Tell us... what are his hobbies?'
'Hobbies? Poets don't have hobbies, they have obsessions.'
'No, no, hob-by, do you understand? Come on, he must have a hobby!'
'Oh yes, yes. He has a hobby; he has been translating the Old Testament into Polish.'

Deadly silence... receiver put down... And then in the final twenty-five years of his life, he became famous, as someone who had lived through so many of the great events of twentieth century, from the Russian Revolution and the Warsaw Ghetto Uprising to the fall of Soviet Communism.

But as Franaszek reminds us, there were other hidden parts of the man. His will to survive. The mask he seemed to wear, already as a student in the 1930s, which served him well under the Communists, twenty years later. And all those women. So many affairs. And perhaps strangest of all that long first marriage. His wife and sons are curious absences throughout the book, popping up here and there. And the devil. Numerous references to Satan. Thinking back to his time in Krakow in 1945, having escaped Warsaw after the Warsaw Uprising, Miłosz wrote, 'There was pleasure in translating Milton in the summer of 1945 in Krakow [...] we were *in patribus deamonis*, and tied to our fate'. It is hard to think of any other modern writer, in their private life or as a witness to historical events, who spent so many years in the provinces of demons. Or who turned these experiences into greater poetry.

From the Archive

Issue 173, January–February 2007

Sujata Bhatt

From a contribution of two poems including 'The Old Man who is Not for Günter Kunert'. Fellow contributors to this issue include Mimi Khalvati, Les Murray, Neil Powell and Jeffrey Wainwright.

Incessant

Incessant, unearthly speech
from creatures so close to the earth –

These night crickets in Caracas –

Mechanical birds, I thought at first,
computer sirena voices –

How I turn and turn
        trying to follow them.

How they interpret and reinterpret Erik Satie –

And they must know Philip Glass –

Precise, constant,
        they take over –
even my private night.

Five Poems*

SUMITA CHAKRABORTY

Bear, II

A bear brings forth her young informous and unshapen.
I now wear the pelt of the conjured beast around my groin.
I think of new words for solace, one of which is knifed.
We take no form until licked into shape by the tongues of those who love us.

And death demands a labor

When it rains in Boston, from each street rises
the smell of sea. So do the faces of the dead.
For my father, I will someday write:
On this day endeth this man, who did all he could
to craft the most intricate fears, this man
whose waking dreams were of breaking the small bones
in the feet of all the world's birds. Father.
You know the stories. You were raised on them.
To end a world, a god dances. To kill a demon,
a goddess turns into one. Almanacs of annihilation
are chronicled in cosmic time. Go on.
Batter everything of mine that you can find.
Find my roe deer with the single antler. Kill him.
Find a girl, or a woman. Display to me her remains
on some unpaved expanse, like road kill
on Kentucky highways, turning from flesh to a
fine sand made of ground bone, under a sun
whose surface reaches temperatures six times hotter
than the finest crematory. On the surface of the earth,
our remains are in unholy concert with the remains
of all who have gone before and all who will follow,
and with all who live. In this way, our ground
resembles a bone house. Search in my body
for my heart, find it doesn't sit gently
where you learned it to be. Thieve in my armory.
Take my saws, take my torches, and drown
my phalanx of bees. Carve into me the words
of the chronicler of hell. Make your very best
catastrophe. My piano plays loud and fast
although my hands are nowhere to be found.
Father, as you well know, I am but a woman.
I believe in neither gods nor goddesses.
I have left my voice up and down the seam
of this country. I, unlike you, need no saws,
or torches. The bees you drowned will come to me
again. Each time you bear your weapons, I,
no more than a woman, grow a new limb.
Each time you use a weapon, my sinews grow
like vines that devour a maple tree.
When I cry, my face becomes the inescapable sea,
and when you drain blood from a creature,
I drink it. On this day this man died,
having always eaten the good food

Hound

Speak to me never again about sacrifice.
Tell me no stories about things left behind.
Should you dream of telling me such a thing
Imagine immediately yourself in front of Orpheus.
Know that for the rest of my life
I do and will name everything Eurydice,
No matter what else I pretend I have named it.
I do not know what my own eyes look like
But often I imagine them like the eyes of a hound
Fresh from the track.
The track, too, is Eurydice.
Each lover. Three dogs. Rose bushes.
My mother, my sister, my home state.
An underground bees' nest. One upright black
   Kawaii piano.
Here are the words you may not speak to me
Because I know them better than you could:
Toil. Sacrifice. Hound. Eurydice.

amid the angry ghosts, having always made
the most overwrought hells.
On this day the moon waxes gibbous
and the moths breed in the old carpets.
On this day from a slit in the ground rises
a girl who does not live long.
On this day to me a lover turns his back
and will not meet my eye.
On this day the faces of the death-marked
are part-willow, part-lion.
On this day has died an artist of ugly tapestries,
and his wares burst into flame.
On this day endeth this man upon who
I hurl the harvest of this ghostly piano,
and on the surface of this exceptional world
the birds have all come to our thresholds,
our windows and our doors, our floorboards,
our attic crannies and underground storerooms,
wires and railroads, tarmacs, highways,
cliffs and oceans, and have all begun to laugh,
a sound like an orange and glittering fire
that originates from places unseen.

Luz

A roe deer   shot in Slovenia
    has a single antler,   looks
like it has just walked   out
    of a fairy   tale, marvels
the hunter,   marvels
    the scientist.   Worlds such as this
were not thought   possible to exist,
    marvels   the astronomer.
No water can   swell
    me or to paste   turn me,
soften   me, no flame
    singes, turns   to ash,
swallows   me, no grist
    makes of me   powder.
The astronomer   is crying.
    The roe deer   was old,
fat   when the hunter
    lit his eye   and his rifle
upon his single horn.   When my eye
    lights on you   I
forget the meaning   of *luz*.
    Or, when my eye   lights on you,
I see only   *luz*.
    These two confessions   mean
the same thing.   In the case
    of this very   untypical and interesting
buck, both   pedicles,
    which should be   separated
grew up together   in one large pedicle.
    Antlers,   like *luz*,
are made from bone.   The mountains
    I visit   are made of my sister's bones
which are much like mine,   but for one
    difference.   Her bone
water   could swell,
    her bone   to paste turned,
her bone truly   singed, to ash,
    swallowed,   turned by grist
to the finest dust.   When my *luz*
    is done for   it is only you
I trust   to see it home.
    In this marvel   of a world
I will wait   for the roe deer.
    I will touch   its velvet.
I will outlast   you.
    I will not   survive you.
These two confessions   mean
    the same thing.   Roe deer
cast aside   their antlers
    each autumn,   having loved them
through every other   season.

Spring

of Moby Dick, and for Bill

I wish to lay before you
a particular, plain statement
whose skeleton we are
briefly to exhibit
out of the trunk,
the branches grow, out of them,
the twigs
chased over the watery
moors, slaughtered
in the valleys oil, and bone
pass unscathed through the fire
and it is only
grey imperfect misty dawn
soon we shall be lost
in its unshored, harborless
immensities that serene
ocean rolled eastwards from me
a thousand leagues of blue and I only
am escaped alone to tell thee
only I am escaped to tell thee.

* These poems appeared in the following journals: 'Bear, II' in *The Journal*, 'And death demands a labor' in *Adroit*, 'Hound' in *Witness*, 'Luz' in *Gulf Coast*, and 'Spring' in *Boston Review*. 'Bear, II' begins with a line from Thomas Browne's *Vulgar Errors*. The title of 'And death demands a labor' comes from Rilke's *Duino Elegies*. 'Spring' is comprised of lines from *Moby Dick*.

Thou Art Translated

FREDERIC RAPHAEL

The Brazen Plagiarist: Selected Poems by Kiki Dimoula,
translated by Cecile Inglessis Mergellos and Rika Lesser (Yale University Press)

'BLESS THEE, BOTTOM! Bless thee! Thou art translated.' Quince's words, at once amiable and mocking, can serve as rubric for any number of discussions on the merits, even the possibility, of successful and/or reliable translation from one language to another. Literature itself is often a form of revision, response at least, within a culture. A 33,333-line sample can be found in Nikos Katzantzakis' sequel to the *Odyssey*. Ought a cross-lingual translator seek to reproduce, as self-effacingly and precisely as possible, the original writer's meaning (but beware the meaning of meaning!) or should she seek to rephrase, even re-imagine, the work had it been composed in the language into which it is being rendered? The crux is at least as old as Richard Bentley (1662–1742), who – as reported by Dr Johnson – somewhat congratulated a new version of the *Iliad* with, 'It's a very pretty poem, Mr Pope, but you must not call it Homer'. In his recently published *The Lesbian Lyre*, however, Jeffrey M. Duban cites Pope's *Iliad* as conspicuously true to the Greek, which is more ominous, perhaps, than conclusive.

What would Bentley have said to Christopher Logue who boasted that knowledge of even a vestige of the original would have blighted the freshness of *his* Homer? Elsewhere, George Steiner saluted Logue's genius with proclamatory guns, but he is quoted here, in Derridan mode, as saying, 'To re-create what has been created so as to affirm, to enunciate its primacy, its seniority of essence and existence, to re-create it in ways which add presentness to presence, which *ful-fil* that which is already complete: this is the purpose of responsible translation.' Janus has spoken.

The loudest modernist drummer for 'creative' translation was, of course, Ezra Pound. His prime example of 'making it new' was in presenting Sextus Propertius in twentieth-century trim: for notorious instance, the Latin word *minas* ('menaces' according to Lewis and Short) was impounded and revised as 'mines', of the Welsh variety. My Cambridge friend, the late John Patrick Sullivan, a Liverpudlian later translated to professorship at U. C. in Santa Barbara, defended Pound against Robert Graves, who became heatedly old school when it came to ol' Ez's rend(er)ing of the classics. Guy Lee, the Latinist who supervised me and Sullivan at Cambridge, took a pragmatic view. In his younger days, he assumed that the happy few at least would enjoy the loose, terse but never casual, way in which he translated Ovid's *Amores* because – with the Latin either in mind or on the facing page – they would read the English as a gloss on, never a substitute for, the original. In later translations, of Virgil and Horace, Guy decided to stick as close to the Latin as possible, since he could no longer presume on the cultural versatility of his reader. He then sought to use no more words or syllables than, in particular, Horace whose metre he also matched.

Vladimir Nabokov was always on the side of fidelity.

Contrary to his own practice *in propria persona*, V. N. translated (even his own early novels?) under the old *New Yorker* slogan 'No fine writing, please'. Deeming 'a pony' the best homage, he boasted that his Englishing of *Eugene Onegin* was a word-for-word, line-for-line reproduction of Pushkin. It was also buttressed by a formidable *apparatus criticus*, detailing Pushkin's debt to French literature. Nabokov's quondam friend and sponsor Edmund 'Bunny' Wilson derided the recherché pedantry which could come of cleaving, supposedly, to the original.

Few storms in the great teacup of literature have raged more tempestuously than the one that swirled around Nabokov's use of 'kinkajou' to translate Pushkin's allusion to a rare breed of small mammal. What could be more intrusively self-admiring than Volodya's 'match' of a carnivorous cat-sized quadruped of central and southern America, of a breed unknown to any common reader (and almost certainly to Pushkin), with whatever the 'equivalent' is in the original? Wilson's own hubris was advertised by going to the mat with a native speaker, but his case was not without merit. Word-for-wordism can procure verbiage into no speakable lingo. The Englished version of Aeschylus's *Agamemnon* by Eduard Fraenkel, a scholar of high quality, was implacably literal in respect of the Greek. Yet who can read a single line out loud without hilarity breaking in? The golden rule in translation is that there is no golden rule.

In an age of cost- and corner-cutting, Yale University Press deserves unalloyed thanks for this fat edition of Kiki Dimoula's poems with the Greek on one page, faced by the English of Cecile Inglessis Margellos and Rika Lesser on the other. Anyone with a smattering of modern Greek can have educative fun looking back and forth in order to see where, as my old schoolmasters used to say, this or that English word or phrase 'came from'. In the Remove at Charterhouse, more than seventy years ago, I translated the Latin word *lupanar* (brothel) as 'stew', a term whose louche meaning I did not know when I purloined it from a Victorian 'pony' – Bohn's classical library – while doing my preparation ('banco' in Carthusian dialect). Bob Arrowsmith, a.k.a. 'The Arrow', eyed me with suspicion, smiled and let the matter pass. The abiding lesson is that, however 'literal', translation involves choices, especially when going from a 'tight' language to the prolific hybrid vocabulary of English.

Plagiary, brazen or covert, is part of the game in low and high circles. Ancient writers conned and pillaged original texts with no scriptural piety. It was not unusual to affect to be translating, citing or improving earlier authors who never, in fact, existed. In the first century AD, the Roman critic Quintilian ironised about those who invent authorities with confidence because 'those who never existed cannot be discovered'. The twentieth-century scholar Felix

Jacoby dubbed such bogus sources as 'Schwindel-literatur'. Nabokov's own *Pale Fire* fashions erudite pyrotechnics in that tradition.

Who nowadays makes much fuss about the accuracy or otherwise of translations of prose works? In some cases – Tom Holland's recent version of Herodotus a brazen instance – up-to-dated jargon leads, here and there, to travesty. In verse, one of the most durably notorious aberrations is the 'objectivist' 1969 version of Catullus by Louis Zukovsky, who preyed on the rhythm and surface of the Latin with swaggering indifference to accuracy. Catullus himself translated Sappho with quasi-camp precision: the Lesbian's girl became Catullus's mistress. What might be a joke verges on outrage when readers lack the resources to gauge the degree of more or less willful distortion.

The young Roman poets whom Cicero categorised as *neoteroi* – innovators and/or kids – took spiritual inspiration from Alexandria, the Hellenic anti-Rome where sophisticated and arcane allusions were trademarks of poets of the school (literally) of Callimachus, for whom big books – not least the epic *Argonautica* of his one-time colleague Apollonius Rhodius – were big shit (*kaka*). Greek poetry has the most deep-rooted family tree, bearing the rarest fruit, of all European verse. There are semi-precious jewels even among the neat anonymous contributors to the Greek Anthology. Greeks go back to go forwards: one line of Kiki Dimoula goes simply 'ê mnêmê, ê mnênê, ê mnêmê' – 'memory, memory, memory'. To remember is the treasury and the blight of the Hellenic Greek.

Seferis, Ritsos and Cavafy – the last Alexandrian before loutish nationalism led to Grexit from his city – are modern instances of poets rendered copiously into other tongues. Marguerite Yourcenar's versions of Cavafy have a loyalty not always to be found in the poet's many other translators. Daniel Mendelsohn, presiding Hellenic pundit of the *New York Review of Books*, is a professor of Greek so feared as to be exempt from cavil: he can translate *okto* (the Greek for 'eight') as 'seven' and still be applauded.

Cavafy – Mendelsohn's *chouchou* – is not regarded with unmitigated reverence in Greece. One cannot call it his native land; he was neither born there nor lived for long, or happily, within its boundaries. His lean poetry can be translated into accessible English (in the first place by Keeley and Sherrard) not least because, so its Greek detractors say, it is often close to prose. George Seferis, the scion of a Greek family evicted from Smyrna in 1922, cosmopolitan diplomat, is less skeletal. Peter Green – one of the greatest Hellenists of our time and a fluent translator from Greek and Latin (at the age of ninetty-two, he is busy on the *Odyssey*) considers Seferis to have been corrupted by undue deference to the school of André Breton. Did Seferis's diplomatic cosmopolitanism have at least something to do with his being awarded the Nobel Prize?

Yannis Ritsos was nothing if not parochial. His output, often in the form of dramatic monologues, gave voice to previously minor mythological characters such as Elektra's sister Chrysothemis. If he owed anything to any foreign influence it was to a romantic, if not Byronic, Marxism. Ritsos was imprisoned several times by the reactionary regimes to which Greece has been submitted in modern times, often with the connivance, if not at the instigation, of European powers and of the US. Nominated six times for the Nobel Prize, he was politically too incorrect to be given it. Kiki Dimoula, whose life as an employee of the Bank of Greece was hardly revolutionary, was also regarded with suspicion by the Colonels, who suppressed the mildly leftist magazine *Kyklos*, to which she was a contributor. They also banned Aristophanes. Greeks regularly meet Greeks.

I have taken a Cavafyan route to the specific case of Kiki Dimoula. In his now anthological *Ithaka*, the Alexandrian encouraged his readers to board Odysseus's slow boat home, enjoying the detours and profiting from dawdles and disasters along the way. Dimoula has rarely left Athens during a long and, in most regards, unadventurous life. She has suffered grief and dislocation, if only by moving from one flat to another, adjacent to the first, and by bereavement. She has taken Apollo's enigmatic advice 'know thyself' (can one?) without lifting her eyes from the familiar and its closely quizzed unfamiliarity. Her unblinking vision transforms the ephemeral into the miraculous, the elusive and, sometimes, the macabre. Unlike her famous quasi-contemporary trio of male poets, Dimoula rarely alludes to antiquity.

In the third century AD, Philostatrus observed, 'For the wise man, Greece is everywhere'. For a wise woman, Dimoula proves, ubiquity can co-exist with never leaving home. She has had to wait till old age (she was born in June 1931) for the honours which might have been delivered more promptly to a male. When inducted into the Athenian academy in 2002, she compared herself, in her speech, to a seemingly one-legged stork she had seen, high up, on the road to Alexandroupolis, in Thrace (I saw one atop the sole remaining pillar of the great temple of Artemis at Ephesus). 'Poetry,' Dimoula said, 'is like a nest to hide in... inaccessible to the rapacious curiosity of anyone who wants to see too clearly what's being hatched inside. The most effective way to safeguard concealment is by subtraction. Art is ever-vigilant, elliptical, balancing on one leg. When we write, we subtract.' The declaration promises obscurities and ellipses to challenge and baffle the literalist. Dimoula's admirer Christophoros Liontakis puts a feathered cap on the problem: 'By glorifying what is apparently insignificant, Dimoula creates a secret poetic theology of ecumenical ramifications.' What is more difficult to convey from one tongue to another than unspoken implications?

The introductory matter in this volume is at once solemn, informative and protracted. The translation was undertaken in unlikely tandem by Cecile Inglessis Margellos, who – as her name promises – is a native Greek speaker and Rika Lesser, whose knowledge of Greek is (or was) limited, she announces, to the letters used in 'chemistry and calculus'. Fie! some might say. I was reminded that, in order to deceive Palamedes into thinking he was mad (and unfit for military service in Troy), Odysseus yoked an ox and a horse to his plough before proceeding to sow salt in his fields. Supplied with a 'pony' by her collaborator, Lesser set herself, braced only with poetic instinct, to anglicise Dimoula. In a prefatory essay entitled 'The Somatics of Semantics', she tells us that, 'It is no secret, or an open one, that I have long been opposed to translating poetry from languages one does not "know".' What do the inverted commas around 'know' tell us that their absence would obscure? Only that Ms Lesser takes herself very seriously: 'There are people for whom the translation of poetry is every bit as creative and essential to their "practice" as writing their own poems.'

The critic Nikos Dimou is quoted as saying that 'every photograph is [...] the presence of an absence [...] The instant dies in the instantaneous snapshot'. If the post-modernist's 'yeah, yeah' comes to mind, photography is a frequent modern *topos* on which Yves Bonnefoy and Wistawa Szymborska – Dimoula's sister in brevity – can be seen to converge. Susan Sontag lent chic to the snapshot in the essay on photography in which she made trendy play with a topic which had illustrations, but no demanding or indecipherable text. Both Bonnefoy and Szymborska can be read in *en regard* editions. A reader with some French, but no Polish, soon appreciates how thoroughly ignorance has to presume on the honesty of the translator (old-style British diplomats took it that there was something shifty about interpreters). Criticism of Dimoula's translators should not detract from gratitude for their brave wrestling with the elusive original. Here, in the way of *mezes* (appetiser and also, in common parlance, teaser), is the first part of *Common Fate*, one of their best, and very good, versions:

My roads
your roads
and this.

He
I
And this

The bridegroom Mays,
The appropriate attire
And this.

The noncombatant feeling,
the hidden knife
and this.

The advancing thirst,
the Samaritan woman
and this.
[...]
Oaths vaulting over time,
the deciduous memory
and this.

Could minimalism get smaller without becoming a void? It should be said that many of the poems do not depend on suggestion to the same extent. Not a few seem less written than inscribed. *Common Fate* (*Tychê Koinê*) illustrates how what cannot be said, without dilation or dilution, remains to be implied. Temples to Fortuna (Latin for *Tychê*) were common in the post-Hellenistic, Romanised Fertile Crescent. *Koinê* is the name regularly given to the lingua franca of the region. Dimoula may not allude directly, or even consciously, to the ubiquity which Philostratus announced, but her language cannot but travel, or

go to war, as she implies in *The Periphrastic Stone*: 'Speak / Words have grudges / engage in rivalries'.

Conscious that those without any modern Greek may be puzzled, if not infuriated, I dare to think that a cull of my six tight pages of notes may, in some cases at least, break through the language barrier and convey both the admiration and the reservations generated during my several readings of this generous selection of remarkable poems. A reader without appetite for detail may choose to alight here, but even those without any Greek may gain a sense of what may be lost, or intruded, in translations.

xxx. Rika Lesser, with no Greek, enrolled as anglicising decorator. xxxiii. Argument re *Aprosdokies* (*hapax*, but found, we are told, in Speusippus's *Platonic Terms*), here rendered 'Nonexpectations', when 'unforeseenities' – making play with obscenities – might have been more fun, because playful like the coinage itself. The solemnity of the debate between the translators makes it clear no spontaneity was ever likely to break through. 'Nonexpectations' doesn't seem a great, or pretty, innovation. Rika Lesser's 'poetic instinct' triumphed over Greek-speaking Cecile. xxxiv. George Steiner cited for his 'ethical stance' xxxv. Girlishly giggling envoi-citing 'jubilating, discreetly crying, and loudly laughing' offers no promise of stylishness. Then: 'The rest is poetry'. If only.

9. Why render *koito* 'before my eyes'? Literally, it means 'I look'. 'I eye' is more fun and implies astonishment. '*Stee dunatee tees korees mesi*' is rendered 'on the girl's strapping waist', a comic and dated phrase which has little to do with the Gk. 'Powerful' won't do, but 'pliant' might; or merely 'strong' (the usual meaning).

11. 'miens' is poeticised and dated. Banalised word order kills the uplift of the last word '*anegeiroun*'. Cavafyan echo here of lost Ithacas?

17. '*dusthumos anemos*' is rendered too poetically as 'a black-browed wind'. Where does 'brow' come from? 'Dispirited' or even 'halitotic' truer and much more fun. '*apo kuria schedon orimee*' is rendered 'by a woman of a certain age', a cliché used for what the Greek plays at not quite saying. 'By a lady all but ripe' is closer; the but plays with 'butt' and suggest amplitude... '*kai cheimones*', key last phrase is singularised and weakened by preposition 'to'. The right procedure might have been to preserve 'And winters' at all costs and fashion the rest to accommodate it.

23. '...exaggeration / ... exaggerating'. No equivalent repeat in Gk, no need in English. Paraphraseology too frequent. 'Personally' too heavy for *ego*.

27. '*s'exakribono mesa mou*' rendered 'I determine that you're inside me'. Surely 'make you out from within myself' (or 'from my inner self') is better than 'determine': it captures the *ex* and the element of accuracy in – *akrib*.

35. Last line '*for it was very great*' ignores Gk word order which can be rendered precisely in English with '*for it was great, very!*' Why flatten into platitude?

41. Word order wrong. *Akopa* can mean 'tirelessly' but only inaccurately: 'ceaselessly' or 'without stopping' is better. How about the 'yearning' Tower of Pisa, to catch *gernei* (pronounced 'yearn-ee' in Greek)?

43. Last line; word order easy to preserve: Bang on time, it's night!

45. Word order. *Apo dtho* is rendered '... from now on'; but 'from here', if not 'from this point on' is more accurate.

50/51. *Synophryose* rendered 'surliness' but etymology

suggests that 'scowl' or 'with knitted brows' truer to the Gk. Lower down, *bios* is rendered 'riches', but 'living' or 'livelihood' stays closer to the text. 'The shots' is too short for *pyrovolismos*, which hints at a 'volley' of shots. 'Take-aim-firing'? We need the 'bang-bang-bang' of the polysyllable.

53. Immediate repetition of 'straight away' ignores the separation of *kateutheian* 1 and 2 in the text, vulgarising the tone. *Stolidzeis kapoio parko* is rendered 'You adorn a park', but 'some park (or other??)' is nicely indefinite, like the Greek.

57. PHOTOGRAPH 1948. Word order wantonly ignored. 'I'm holding a flower, probably' is better than, 'I'm probably holding a flower', which is bad English and fails to enjoy the oddity of reading a photo as if unsure of its precise content. Can happen, but the printed version doesn't convey this ambiguity.

72/3. Good work. But 'third-rate' for *psoros* is lazy because without nuance: 'mingy' or 'sickening', 'unhealthy', 'spotty' even hints at the psoriatic root of the matter...

78. Good re 'Words hold grudges' etc.

84/85. Last words on page *'kai perimenei'* rendered 'and waits'; 'and hangs about' echoes the Greek prefix *peri* and has a taste of modish slang.

127. Nice, but why tr. *Zoerochroma* 'brightly coloured' when, in a chemist shop context, the *zoe-* deserves preservation, banal if necessary, as in 'lively coloured' (contrast with next stanza and its poison)?

162. Why render *'hemiteles'* as 'unfinished' when it has to mean half-finished? Latter tr is in lexicon, but it's lazy, if not inaccurate.

178. *Malakio* (mollusc) is first word in 2nd stanza, line one, relegated to last in tr. Wrong!

192. SAINT LAZARUS' DAY. Last stanza disordered has no piquancy. Should end, 'That bed of theirs'.

200. *Exallou as mên krubomaste* is rendered, 'Besides, let's be frank', but 'Anyway, let's not conceal it' is closer to what it says.

211. *Ekrêtikos* does mean 'explosive' but the mention of Icarus is picked up by the false (?) etymology which gives the word the shadowy etymology 'ek-Kretes', from Crete. Word order not respected.

215. THE ALMOND TREE'S CARNIVAL. Very good.

218. *'phtochos'* means 'poor' not 'no'.

222. SHAKE WELL BEFORE USING. V.g. *'akumantê'* is rendered, correctly, 'waveless'; but 'unwavering' wd be more fun and true to the case, where 'waveless' says nothing pertinent to the (Hesiodic?) 'works and days'.

225. 'split' superfluous and spoils the profligate nature of the gale that does not discriminate between branches and ears.

230. Poor tr. of *'adunatidzei'* as 'grows dim', when 'loses its force' is better and truer.

238. First line word order kills the emphatic opening *'Ekklêsia'*. Cf. Juan Ramon Jimenez' *'Catedral del sur...'*

246. 'Why can't you ever be a liar?' is more to the point. I don't see 'for once' in the text.

284. *'to choma mou pephtei baru'* is translated 'Dirt is too great a burden'. Literally, it's 'Earth falls heavy on me'. To miss out 'me' generalises the particular. See also maladroit first line, 'enmity' isn't right either.

300. Why 'How I wish' when the Greek says, 'How I have wished'? There is a difference.

302. *kompiasma* is rendered 'Hemming and hawing' (as in the lexicon), but one word for one word is better surely, e.g. 'Dithering'. Also 'unpredictable' is better than 'in all kinds of...' for *aschetôs*.

304. *'Katadzêtoumai'* is rendered 'I'm wanted by the police'; but the police are not mentioned in the Greek which means, 'I am being looked for'; perhaps 'I'm on the wanted list' (one word for one word won't do the work here). Last line *'egô den agoradzo'* is rendered 'no sale', but the Greek says and the sense requires, 'Me, I'm not buying'. Since *egô* is not necessary to the syntax, the 'I' has to be emphatic, not suppressed.

From the Archive

Issue 1, October–December 1977

CHARLES BOYLE

From a contribution of four poems ('Foreign', 'The Poverty of Romanticism' and 'Au Café'). The issue also features poems by Donald Davie and C. H. Sisson, an essay by Octavio Paz on Solzhenitsyn and Neil Powell appraising the poetry of Peter Scupham.

ARABIA SUBURBIA

Hourly, hourly, the city blunders out –
a desert yields to concrete, the kids
race bikes between the faceless blocks.

With fans and drinks to cool the noon
the women sleep, their men play chess,
this calm asylum of the rich and mild.

The dogs roam, they scratch for scraps.
Indifferent by day, at night
the meanest scent will make them bark,

their bark will then awake me:
from the rooftop now you can see
small fires, can smell the farther sand.

Two Poems

LORNA GOODISON

Ireland Jamaica

My friend Dan O'Riley Kelly's skin is the colour of a glass of Guinness.
A wild man who once locked four of us in his car one Monday
and drove us through ink-dark Bog Walk's carbon cachement
across low and precarious Flat Bridge, to a dirty dive of a night club
that as it turns out had been closed down. So right there in the empty
asphalt carpark under the light of a tinnin moon, he danced by his own
self, as we sulked and allowed as how the next day was a workday
and we'd been dragged miles away on a fool's errand; and that made
him laugh the more as he did his own peculiar roots-reggae riverdance
to the hind-leg rubba dub riddim of tree crickets. When he did take us
home past cane flags pennanting in the night wind, he urged us to sing
along to a maddening mixed tape he'd made from twelve terribly strange
instrumental bootleg versions of 'raindrops keep falling on my head'.

Funeral In Knockpatrick

Rice-white blossoms blew from a tree by the room's one window
and settled upon the corpse laid out in an open coffin.
Funeral confetti or light food shared and eaten in haste at the last?
No one I asked knew what the name of the tree was.

A brown man dressed in a black suit; he sported a grey moustache,
his white shirt pearl-buttoned up to the neck. He had a half-
smile on. I was there because his daughter was a courtesy aunt,
her name was Maude. Maybe her Father had christened her

after Yeats's great love; except I do not recall her as beautiful.
For sure no one would write her poems; except her own father,
the dead man who was mostly Irish, and who had the look of a poet.
Don't ask me why I say this, I was after all only a nine-year-old girl

who saw a man lying in state in a house in red-dirt Knockpatrick.
A man I'd never known in life; but who looked to be at peace,
his face clean, as the blossoms blown in from a tree – the name of which
I'll know one day – dusted him there in his plain pine coffin.

Two Poems

Theophilus Kwek

Westminster

22 March 2017

I

Broken light, high water. Here and elsewhere
the cold thought of something beyond belief
settling into movement – an unstoppable design –
lodges in the throat, will not be sung.
We fall on words made for other means:
Visibility, four miles. More clouds than sun.

II

Within days, it seems, this injury
will join the rim of that other, deeper cut
over which no scar can form. Unclean, unshut.
As yet it gapes distinct: flesh wound, a loss
without name and yet no easier
to reckon, its surface so bare of facts
except the act of loss itself, no choice
or distance, no motive, no face, no legend,
(a mere expanse which holds the skin apart)
no way to map the way to map a way.

III

Lines open for interchange. The earth trembles,
holds fast this steel heart, its brave circulation.
Every safe passage a jubilee. Who are they
whose paths must cross at our deepest station?

IV

Already, without doubt, we have begun to fear
and fear the upshot of fear, the lightning and the storm.
But darkness now, which passes for calm.
                                        A prayer:

V

For each morning that takes place unawares.
The still scalding shower. The flight of stairs.

What It's Like*

How do I tell you now about the way
they placed it in his hands, a baby's weight,
just as tenderly pulled his shoulders back
to take the heave and coil, every fresh blow
leaving him sore, the sour echo of *this
is how you kill a man?*
                    *It takes a man
to do that for his country,* they said, and there
in the wet scrape it seemed almost true,
knowing a body's length of new earth lay
upturned, packed tight to rest his barrel on,
not daring to move, legs and torso stained
with an afternoon's digging, as ten a time
slipped away to practise advancing
from point to point, or picking up the dead,
the whole earth shattering beneath them.
Don't be scared,
              these aren't even live.
He learned to play dead, always the lightest
in the group, the one his friends would plan
to evacuate, arms crossed over one
another's to stabilise the casualty, last man
claiming his rifle where it fell *so we don't
give the rascals anything.*
                    *If you're lucky,
he's still breathing* (and always, the refrain)
if not, don't move him.
                    It's hard to tell
the truth of it – even half, he thinks – but these
are the things he knew, or maybe knows now,
or wishes he did, is what I'm saying.

---

* First published online in the *Asia Literary Review*,
June 2017.

Three Poems

MARY JEAN CHAN

Three Sonnets: Versions from the *Twenty-Four Filial Exemplars*

Èrshísì Xiào or the *Twenty-Four Filial Exemplars* is a classic text of Confucian filial piety written during the Yuan Dynasty (1260–1368), and has been used as an example of how Chinese children should honour their parents.

He Lay Down on Ice in Search of Carp

One of the strangest, this: how a boy mistreated
by his stepmother still tried to satisfy her cravings
for carp, sought out the frozen lake and thawed the ice with
naked flesh, brought home two pregnant ones
for a pot of soup. At eight, I learnt this fable from
my mother's lips, offered immediately to out-do this filial son,
though there was no ice to be found all across the city –
our temperate winters incapable of frost.
Years later, I wonder why my mother did not mention
hypothermia or the possibility of drowning, did not
invite me to wonder at the boy's lack
of self-respect, did not consider how his body
deserved its own morsel of warmth, how his fingers
should never have been bait.

He Fed the Mosquitoes with His Blood

Another begins with a sacrifice: a boy too poor
to afford mosquito nets offers his blood as nectar in his parents'
stead, as he sits on their bed on hot summer nights to keep
them safe from the unbearable scorch
of inflamed skin. I read this alone as a teenager,
my Chinese now oxidised as black tea, capable
of steeping in fabled warnings. Once more, I detect
how dispensable the child's body is, how right it is that he
suffers for an ideological wound, how his parents
might have slept fitfully that night, roused by their child's
cries as the mosquitoes encircled him, or perhaps
blinking back a tear while thinking how good
their boy is, how proper this bloody
business of proving one's love.

He Dressed Up to Amuse His Parents

No longer a boy, but an old man, dressed up
as a child to amuse his elderly parents, his fists
adorned with toys: a wooden stick, a piece of polished
stone. This isn't the worst fable amongst the twenty-
four, but it makes me rage, because I am now
twenty-four, no longer in need
of dolls, though my mother yearns
for my feet to shrink to the size of her
open palms, and for the rest
of me to follow. Some days I cannot be her
child again, although I pacify arguments
and tears with a playful voice
that pleases, if only to reassure her –
and to say that love
is patient, love is kind.

respite

father slept
in the living room

to spare mother
a common cold

she coughed anyway
bereft on the silent bed

unsure of which way
to turn in the dark

mother asks: will you lie
next to me, just for tonight?

i said i would, sliding
into my father's skin

she slips into slumber
my head resists the pillow

as i toss and turn
into daylight.

Long Distance

Your call tears me from my past into your present.
You ran till your feet sang on the rain-dark pave-
ment, till you outpaced rhythm and thunder. All
the dehumidifiers are on in the house. No fireplac-
es. Some seas are colder than others, some bodies
warmer. I am drinking Iron-Buddha: two teabags
waiting for their time to blossom. It is too Spring
here for my own good; too much green in the salad
bowl. Too many stories of salvation; earlier, blue
beyond belief. The moon is lying on its back in
my dreams. What a smile looks like. A toothbrush
touches my lips. Asian steamed sea bass for din-
ner, with white rice. Polar bears have black skin.
Victoria Harbor was named after your Queen. How
many hearts in a deck of cards shuffled across two
continents? I am catching a plane tonight, thinking
about the map on your neck. *Roaming.*

A Cuban View of Hemingway

MARIO MENOCAL & JEFFREY MEYERS

MARIO MENOCAL'S GRANDFATHER had been a
general in the Cuban war of independence against
Spain and president of the country from 1913 to
1921. Mario's wealthy, cultivated and aristocratic
father, Mayito, was educated at Lawrenceville School
and Cornell University, and became Hemingway's
sporting companion and best Cuban friend. While
fishing in the Caribbean on Mayito's large yacht,
Delicias, they would discuss pigeon shooting, jai alai,
current books, local gossip, Cuban affairs and world
politics while drinking gin with champagne chasers.
Mayito went on Hemingway's wartime sub-hunting
expeditions, which he called a 'stunt', and accom-
panied him on his second African safari in 1953.
Mayito's son Mario – born in 1923, twenty-four years
younger than Hemingway and the same age as his
oldest son, Jack – was also educated in America.
When Fidel Castro's revolution in 1960 drove his
family into exile, they lost their valuable sugar
business, house and possessions. After leaving Cuba,
Mario became an executive with PepsiCo and other
companies, and a Spanish translator in Mexico City
and Miami.

An eager and generous correspondent, Mario had
ample opportunity to closely observe Hemingway
and his elite circle of Cuban friends from 1940 to
1960. His letter of 18 April 1983 – elegantly composed,
intelligent and perceptive – is the best one ever writ-
ten about Hemingway. He is especially acute about
Hemingway's puritan character, relations with his son
Gregory, African safari, sub-hunting in the Second
World War and disastrous love for Adriana Ivancich
as well as Martha Gellhorn's provocative flirtations
and Mary Welsh's alcoholism. We disagreed about
some important points, and I later found proof from
Jane Mason's diary and interviews with her family
that she *had* been Hemingway's lover. But Mario's
valuable insights enabled me to test and develop
my ideas as I was researching and writing my life of
Hemingway, published by Harper & Row in 1985.

18 April 1985
Dear Professor Meyers:

THE AFRICAN SAFARI. My father told me pretty
nearly everything about his safari with E. H. It was the
best time he ever had in his life. He had been looking
forward to it since his childhood, and in his later years
I think we talked as much about that as we did about
all other subjects put together. He was sad and lonely
after he left Cuba, he knew he didn't have long to live,
and nostalgia was a refuge and a solace for him.

Ernest was a good enough hunter during the *Green Hills* safaris; in the later one, he was quite simply afraid of shooting too badly, of making a spectacle of himself, which is something that, if circumstances dictate, can happen even to the world's champion rifle shot. You will have noted how conscious (and admiring) I've always been of the efforts Ernest invariably made to create and sustain the image he had deliberately built up in the mind of the public. I think his fear was of damaging that image in the presence of a potentially hostile stranger. And in this case the stranger could only have been Earl Theisen as he was the only outsider, and he was an outsider who worked for a *photo magazine and had a camera.*

I don't believe Ernest could have been afraid of the animals. He was physically courageous (no one who knew him ever doubted that); and he wasn't a rookie, he'd shot lion and rhino and buffalo before. Even if he had been a physical coward (and I'm making this speculation merely for the sake of demonstration, and not because I'm willing to believe he may have been one), he was much too intelligent not to be absolutely certain that, backed by Philip Percival, Roy Home, and my father (who was an even better shot than the professionals), he would have been in no danger at all. His fear was of making a public mess of things and thereby transmitting his image in Ty's presence. Had it not been for my father's constant intervention, I believe the safari would have ground to a dead stop and there could even have been a lawsuit, or at least very bad feelings between Ernest and *LOOK.* Perhaps you have or can get the *LOOK* cover of Ernest with a leopard: that leopard, and almost every other animal shown in the *LOOK* articles, was shot by my father.

MARTHA'S FLIRTATION WITH FELIX AREITIO. She had a heavy flirtation – I don't think it was ever an affair, but it was certainly past the point to which a flirtation should have been taken, with the man you inquire about. His name was Felix Aréitio, he was a Basque, then in his late twenties, from the village of Ermua, and (as so many *pelota* players do), he used the name of his village as his 'nom de jeu'. He was a very good jai-alai player, the second-best in the world in the position he played (there are only two in *pelota*: 'delantero', forward, who covers the front part of the court, and 'zaguero', back, who covers the rear); 'Ermua' was a 'zaguero'. If I had been Ernest I would have objected to the physical familiarities Martha and Felix allowed themselves – yet it was precisely those physical familiarities which convinced me then and continue to convince me now that there was never an affair between them. 'Physical familiarities' sounds worse than it was, like 'expletive deleted' in the Nixon transcripts; they were never anything shocking, really, but rather unusual and unexpected: for example, Martha jumping into Felix's arms at the tennis-court so he would have to carry her up the hill to the house instead of her having to walk – nothing could be more banal in 1983, but we are speaking of 1940 or thereabouts, and of relations between a sophisticated and extremely liberated American woman, and a very good-looking Basque peasant who happened to be a very good *pelota*-player. I consider it perfectly understandable that neither Martha nor Ernest should have

realized that she shouldn't indulge in such behavior. That's the answer to 'why did he tolerate it?'

DID I EVER SEE E.H. DRUNK? Only slightly less frequently than I saw him sober. Belligerent or fighting? He had a quick temper and pet hates, and bitterly resented intrusion, particularly when he believed the intruder was seeking personal benefit. That made him very angry; and he became belligerent (but not to the point of physical violence) when angry. I never saw him fight; in fact, I never saw him even come near to a fight, in all the years I knew him. I don't think any of his other older friends ever saw that either.

MY EXPERIENCES WITH ERNEST. I understand him and his motivations better after having read *A Moveable Feast.* I find many things that he did and wrote much easier to understand after having learned from his own lips (so to speak) about his guilt at allowing himself to be seduced by Pauline and by the life she could give him. I don't think he ever got over that, nor that he ever felt that any of the wives who came after Hadley were (*qua* wives, not *qua* lovers) deserving of the same treatment that Hadley would have had from him had he remained married to her.

ADRIANA IVANCICH. Her character: that of a charming, intelligent, gifted member of the Venetian establishment. Supremely worldly and sophisticated, even at the age of 19 or 20 as she was in the Hemingway period. Very good-looking, super-sexy in a very Italian way.

The following is very little known: Adriana was sincerely in love with Juan Veranes, and they were to be married. Adriana didn't have a nickel, and when she and Juan agreed that he would arrive in Paris to go from there to Venice to marry her, on a specific date by a specific flight of a specific airline, she was absolutely sure that he would do so, and therefore she and Gianfranco and the rest of the family got together every penny they could scrape up to finance Gianfranco's automobile trip to Paris to pick Juan up and take him to Venice for the wedding. Imagine the general feeling in the Ivancich family when Gianfranco spent the entire day at the Paris airport and Juan never showed up.

What happened was that Juan met another European girl, a Spanish one called Angelita Osborne, from one of the well-known sherry-growing families of Jerez – and he transferred his attentions (and spent all the money he had scraped together for the trip to Venice) on Angelita, and turned his back without a qualm on the promises he had made to Adriana.

It makes me sad for her as she was then, and even sadder when I remember that she committed suicide just a few days ago. Poor Adriana, so full of life and beauty, so bright and clever and witty: I would never have imagined such an end for her, and regret it, and the unhappiness it reflects, most deeply.

I don't think Ernest ever knew of the relationship between Juan and Adriana. However, I think Mary did know of it, and fostered it, logically so: it was another way of getting Adriana out of her life, and of getting Ernest to cease to make a spectacle of himself.

34–35

Poems

Chan

Features

Menocal

& Meyers

SUB-HUNTING. There are two aspects of this. The first is what we, his friends, believed. We believed that it was a gimmick he had invented so that he and Winston Guest and Paxtchi Ibarlucia and the other members of the sub-hunting crew could continue fishing without worrying about gasoline. Do I still believe that? Not as strongly as I did at the time, for the following reasons which as you will see have nothing to do with the morality or lack of it in the activity. We knew nothing whatever of what Ernest was actually doing, except what he told us. But Ambassador Spruille Braden did, and so did the Naval Attaché, who was a Marine, Lt. Col. John W. Thomason Jr. Neither of those men was stupid, nor is it probable that both of them would have been so dazzled by the Hemingway aura as to permit such an obvious swindle as the sub-hunting would have been if it was merely an artifice conceived to permit E. H. to continue fishing and being an 'ocean bum' (his term), undisturbed by the war.

From another and perhaps equally valid point of view, the consumption of gasoline by the *Pilar*, even had she remained at sea for 24 hours a day, 12 months a year, would have been so insignificant, as viewed by someone in Braden's or Thomason's position, as to lead him to say to himself, 'what the hell, I have to authorize thousands of gallons for crooked Cuban politicians and military and naval officers to sell on the black market; Ernest is a great American, I'll let him have all the gas he wants, and if he ever spots a sub, great, and if he doesn't, it will be so many gallons the Cuban pols didn't get their hands on.'

And that is what I think now.

I also think that Ernest would never tell himself the truth about his activity. He must have realised that, even if he had spotted a sub, what could he have done, except radio to US naval vessels that were too far away to do anything about it? Did he seriously think that a German sub would allow a fishing boat such as the *Pilar* to approach to close quarters? It would have machine-gunned him to Kingdom Come! Ernest must have known that, and I don't think he or any member of his crew had any sort of Kamikaze mentality or intention.

AMBASSADOR BRADEN'S REPUTATION with Cubans, as I remember it, was that of a blowhard and blusterer. Some people say he was a very shrewd businessman, or had been, in Peru; others said that he had very little or nothing to do with Braden Copper. My feelings, for what they are worth, were that the US Ambassador was the second (or first) most important man in Cuba, and whether the US sent us a complete asshole – as they did on many occasions – or a WASP so wrapped up in his own Waspishness that he could never be expected to understand a Latin American, even a Cuban mentality, (we got some of those, too) or a truly competent man (and there were also some of those) – there he was: the US Ambassador and we had to live with him.

E.H.'S FRIENDSHIP WITH GUSTAVO DURAN. I am delighted to have read (in your article) that he was investigated by the State Department, cleared, and had a distinguished career in the UN. Mr Durán's successful record delights me for two reasons. One, it is another item of evidence that E. H. was the patriotic American we always knew him to be. Two, it emphasises once again Ernest's ability as a picker.

MANUEL BENITEZ. I know him well; he is very much alive, and saw him often. He was and is a *dreadful* man, although sometimes a very comic one. Let me see how well I can describe him to you.

His history is very simple. His father was a Colonel who became political boss in Pinar del Río province, and got his son appointed to the Cuban equivalent of West Point. When Batista and the other army sergeants revolted, Manuel Benítez (then a recently graduated lieutenant) was one of the three officers who threw in their lot with the sergeants. Batista rewarded him for this by making him a Colonel (the highest rank there was, after the 1933 revolt), and subsequently Chief of Police. In both positions his name was a synonym for graft.

He was always a slightly pudgy man, and his looks were a perfect caricature of the standard 'Latin Lover' type: black hair, swarthy skin, handsome in a coarse way.

I suppose his outstanding characteristic was his absolute, utter lack of shame. He is the sort of man who openly acknowledges being the worst sort of thief and grafter, and sincerely believes that if you are not one it is because you've never had the opportunity. He carried this belief to the extent of telling anecdotes of events (about Batista, for example) when he (Benítez) held office. They were most interesting and funny, both because Manolo is a very funny person, and because of the utter shamelessness with which he relates an anecdote, with himself as protagonist, that another man would pay blackmail to keep secret.

However, despite his comic side, I believe him to be fundamentally an evil man who would commit any crime, and may have committed many, without the slightest compunction.

JANE MASON. You say that 'it now seems clear' that Jane Mason was E. H.'s 'mistress' from about 1932–36. I don't believe Jane and Ernest ever had an affair. On the other hand, I would lay odds that she and Sánchez did have one. My reasons for believing as I do are twofold. The first is Ernest. He wasn't an 'affair' man: I don't think he knew how to conduct one. When he went from one sexual partner to another, it was from a wife to a woman he intended to make his wife. He always wanted to get married and stay married. None of us, especially not my father or Elicio (who, I repeat, were his best friends, and the latter of whom was additionally his most assiduous companion except for stooges), ever mentioned Ernest's name in connection with that of Jane Mason. And they did mention her name in connection with others, especially with Thorwald.

RELATIONSHIPS BETWEEN E. H. AND HIS SONS. While they were under college age, they were very good. After that they seemed to spoil – I wasn't around very much just then, so I don't know exactly how or why. By the way, Patrick is *not* exactly my age: Bumby is. I will be 60 on 16 June.

GREGORY HEMINGWAY. I ceased to see Gigi many years before I left Cuba. I am quite a lot older than he, and although I suppose it wouldn't make a great deal of difference now, when I am 59 and he is (I suppose) in his early fifties, as it did when I was 20 and he was 14 or 15 or even younger. I don't know his exact age.

We all liked him very much. He was lively, clever, witty, and seemed wise beyond his years. He was a very good shot, as was Patrick, but Gigi was more notable because he was younger and quite small in size. Patrick came to stay with me at Santa Marta, after I was married, and I think greatly enjoyed himself. I don't know why Gigi didn't come. I have only two sources of information about Gigi, after I ceased to see him: Mary – it was she who told me, on more than one occasion, that Gigi was a transvestite – and Gigi's own book about himself.

Then later I read Gigi's book, which didn't really cast a lot of light on his life when I knew him; except he wrote that in those days when he wasn't even in his teens, he had frequently been drunk. If he has suffered all the troubles you say, poor Gigi, especially alcoholism, certainly no small part of them must be due to his unorthodox childhood. To your question of whether I believe Ernest was responsible for Gigi's condition I must reply that of course he must have been, in good part. Until I read Gigi's book I believed that Ernest had been a very good father to his children until their late teens but after I read it, I began to wonder.

By the way, when I say 'his children', I mean Patrick and Gigi – Bumby was Mrs Hadley Mowrer's child, he wasn't under Ernest's influence one percent as much as the younger children, nor did he ever participate (except for very brief periods) in the life with Ernest in Cuba. Later, after Bumby was married, he did come to Cuba to live. I think he worked for Merrill Lynch while he was there. But we disliked his wife, so saw very little of him. I don't think he saw a great deal of his father even when he lived in Cuba, but I was away most of the time, so I can't state that as a fact.

ERNEST AS A CATHOLIC. As far as I knew, his family was Protestant, and although I know that Ernest spoke of himself as a Catholic, I think he became one when he married Pauline. I should rather say that *he* said that he became one; Ernest was no more a Catholic than he was a Moslem. As religion is one of my least favorite subjects for conversation or reading, you will understand that I have never given much more thought than as expressed above to Ernest's religion or lack of it.

PAULINE AND MARY. I believe that the basis for the later friendship of Pauline and Mary is as follows. Patrick had a serious motorcycle accident. He was very ill indeed, and it was thought best that Pauline come down to take care of him. Of course she stayed at the Finca, as Mary's guest. Neither woman had any reason to resent the other, and they were both good persons. I suppose they liked each other, and became friends. This is surmise, as I wasn't in Havana while Mouse was ill and his mother was there.

I can't compare their intelligence because I never knew Pauline. I would say (from photographs) that as far as looks were concerned, Mary was far superior.

MARY AND ALCOHOL. Mary *did not* drink heavily (in fact she drank very little) when she married Ernest. I can only recall seeing her drunk on occasions when everyone else, the undersigned very much included, was drunk too. She was more a party drinker than anything else. In later life (in late widowhood), she began to drink more than was good for her, and I think I know the reason. Mary is a very strongly sexed woman, and could not stand the absence of a man in her life. In fact, I would attribute her present alcoholic condition to her inability to resign herself to age and the concomitant loss of feminine attraction, and therefore of masculine companionship. I realize this may be an oversimplification – but am sure that her inability so to resign herself is at least one of the principal reasons for her present state.

I regret very much having had the misfortune to see Mary when she was falling or had fallen into her present condition. For eight years before I began my present business, in 1975, I was employed by PepsiCo and travelled frequently to New York. I never failed to call Mary, and she always found something pleasant for us to do together; on one occasion she invited me to see the play 'Hair', which she detested, but I liked; on another she and I and the former (and late) Ilka Chase and her husband went to some sort of function at the Museum of Natural History. This was in addition to my visiting her at her apartment, simply so that we could bring each other up to date on each other and on mutual friends. We usually had at least one meal at Voisin, which was across the street from her apartment. But in 1975 I quit Pepsi and therefore ceased to travel to New York with any frequency. When I was last there, I hadn't seen Mary for a long time. I was staying with my nephew and thought that it would be a good thing to take him to meet Mary, and I did so. Although it was only noon, she was absolutely drunk, more so than I had ever seen her and drunk the way alcoholics get drunk. I made the visit as brief a one as I could, and was very sorry that I had gone. A year or two later I had occasion to use the services of her lawyer, Alfred Rice, and asked him if I should go and see her. He recommended that I don't, saying that five minutes after I had left, she wouldn't remember that I'd been there. He was very sad for her, as was I. By no means did that begin with Ernest, nor was it due to him. He can be blamed for many things, but *emphatically* not for poor Mary losing her memory and becoming an alcoholic. Please be assured that although in 1975 (fourteen years after Ernest's death) Mary may have drunk more than she did during Ernest's lifetime, in no way could she have been considered an alcoholic. I can't say when things changed, but it was after that date.

SLIM HAYWARD. I did know her, although I only saw her on two or three occasions. I always thought she was more Mary's friend than Ernest's. They were thrown together a lot when *The Old Man and the Sea* was being filmed and Hayward visited Cuba, although Slim returned on her own, later, to go fishing with

Ernest and Mary and Elicio Arguelles. Come to think about it, I actually met Slim long before that: I met her many years before, when she was married to Howard Hawks, and Ernest was either married to or about to marry Martha. I think it must have been when *For Whom the Bell Tolls* was about to be filmed.

Slim was very tall and slim, and she was one of the most flat-chested women I've ever seen, but quite attractive despite that. She was also very famous for her good taste in dress, and was on the list of 'ten best-dressed women' for many years. I didn't know her well enough to form any opinion about her intelligence, but she was very quick and clever and pleasant to talk to, and she married two of the biggest powerhouses in Hollywood, so she must have had something besides looks, as she couldn't compete with movie stars as far as looks were concerned.

Where do you get these rumors about women being sexually involved with Ernest? That's not the sort of man he was at all. I don't care what kind of letters Slim says she has, I don't believe there was ever anything between them.

Can it be possible that a number of women, who never in their lives had anything to do with Ernest sexually, are now saying that they slept with him? I imagine it is a distinction of a sort, but not one I would have said that Slim Hayward or Jane Mason would ever have sought, especially in old age.

BUCK LANHAM. I'm not surprised to learn that he was a puritan. He was a true American gentleman, the best type of pre-WWII US Army officer – I can only wish for the sake of the US that its present Army had more Buck Lanhams. However, Ernest wasn't really a coarse-spoken person, and I can't see why Buck should have been offended by his speech, but I do quite understand that he must had been put off by E.H.'s behavior, which could certainly be boorish and inconsiderate, especially when he had been drinking too much for too long. I can also perfectly understand Mrs Lanham (whom I never met) being offended by Ernest's attitude towards women. Ernest didn't understand women and wasn't really very good at relations with them. His Cuban friends, who were in any case absolute epitomes of male chauvinist piggishness, solved that problem very simply: their wives rarely saw or consorted with E.H.

By the way, that aspect hurt Mary very much. She minded the fact that all of Ernest's Cuban friends visited her house but she was never asked to theirs. I don't understand why her closest friends (my father and Elicio) didn't explain to her that, in my father's case, he and my mother separated (although they never got a divorce, and continued to live under the same roof) in 1935, and never had any sort of social life after that; while in Elicio's case, his marriage went through hell for years before it achieved any stability, and neither did he and his wife ever do any entertaining.

You ask what, apart from war experiences, was the basis for the Hemingway–Lanham friendship. I don't think there was any other basis than that. They met during the war, became friends, went through bad times together (and Buck especially appreciated that, because Ernest didn't have to go through them), and

that was enough for the friendship, as it has been for so many others.

OAK PARK PURITANISM. You refer, by implication, to E.H., the simple boy from Oak Park, let loose in Havana, one of the 'sin capitals of the world'. It is quite true that *au fond* Ernest was the son of Dr and Mrs Hemingway from Oak Park, with the moral background they taught him. It is also quite true that Havana was one of the 'sin capitals of the world'. But the juxtaposition of Ernest and Havana, even as seen by ourselves (in our standing – similarly implicit in your query – of supreme sophisticates) didn't work out in the way you appear to imply.

Please ask yourself the following question, as I have asked it of myself so many times. If there is one city in the world that has always been considered the 'Sin Capital', it is Paris. Why then, is the question you ask about Ernest and Havana never asked about him while in Paris, or while he was in Rome and other Italian cities, despite the fact that he was much younger and therefore much more likely to fall into temptation?

Ernest had the ethics and morals of an American of the middle class. Our ethics and morals were those of Cubans (the generalisation 'Latin Americans' isn't specific enough) of the privileged class. To reduce to essentials something that could very easily turn into a hundred-page disquisition, essentially the main differences between the two codes of ethics – as practised, not as taught – lie in the field of sexual morality.

Yet when Ernest diverged from the straight and narrow path in that area, he didn't do so in the ways we, his Cuban friends did. Never for a single moment did Ernest forego American middle class morality for the life of a swinging Latin American playboy. Nothing can be further from what he actually did. When he forewent US middle-class morals it was *to adopt US privileged-class morals*. Let me rephrase that. When Ernest broke the code of sexual morals he had been taught, it was not through the sort of break that one of us would have committed: it was through the sort that people of Winston's and Tommy's sort would commit.

I don't believe any of the biographers or essayists who have written of Ernest have attached sufficient importance to, or described in detail, the process whereby he discarded the normal avocations of middle-class America (for example, team sports) and adopted those of the leisured class (for example, big game fishing and shooting). I believe his liking for bullfighting should also be considered a leisured-class avocation *for and as among Anglo-Saxons*; your ordinary American small-town man boy of the twenties and thirties knew nothing about bullfighting and cared less.

Despite Ernest's contemptuous reference to 'Porcellianed, Skull-and-Bones-ed' spectators of bullfighting (in *Death in the Afternoon*, look it up), such spectators were much more likely to be the sort of people among whom members of Porcellian or Skull and Bones were to be found, than Americans of any other class; and for good reason: travel to Spain cost money.

And when Ernest took up American leisure-class avocations, he also adopted American leisure-class morals. If his sins could have spoken they would have done so in upper-class Eastern US accents, as opposed to middle-class Middle Western ones – and by no stretch of the imagination would they have had done so in the accents of 'señoritos madrileños' or of Cuban swingers.

Why has none of the experts on Hemingway ever examined or commented on this aspect of his character?

Why did Ernest choose all his intimate friends, almost without exception, from the privileged class? Buck Lanham is an exception, but there are very few others. And even Buck Lanham was a member of an elite: within the US Army he was a marked man, an only slightly junior member of the group of officers who were marked for stardom, for the top jobs, after the Marshalls and Eisenhowers and Bradleys retired.

Ernest was not a Puritan, except to the extent that all middle-class Americans of his generation were, to the same extent that Puritanism was present in the morals of middle-class Americans born around the turn of the century.

38–39
Features
Menocal
& Meyers
Poems
Burrows

We Cubans were quite familiar with American middle-class morality. We worked and played with Americans, all our lives; how could we be unfamiliar with it? There was nothing mysterious or strange or different about it; it was the way Americans thought and lived and acted. Their ways would never be ours, nor would ours ever be theirs, even if we lived a thousand years – but that didn't mean there was anything strange about them.

HEMINGWAY AND THE FBI. Finally, you cannot imagine how deeply I have been angered – even more deeply as it is an anger fueled by impotence – by your revelations that the FBI *was in fact* pursuing Ernest when he was hopelessly ill. That damage is done; Ernest took his own life, and as the criminal arrogance of FBI and the stupidity of his physician contributed to his suicide, I'm very glad you've made it public.

Sincerely,
M. G. Menocal

I'll See Myself Out

MILES BURROWS

Some poets lift you up.
Others let you down.
Most leave you exactly where you were.
I'm reading the banker poets.
The banker poets write with prescience
And the self-knowledge and guilt of bankers,
And they are writing for other bankers.
I don't mean the tailored girls waiting to help you with the computer in the wall
Beneath the giant replay of the football match of Everton vs Spurs
I don't mean the pretty Czechs or the wide-eyed Irish colleens
Like hostesses in a plane not wobbling
But staying up on faith alone without us having to concentrate.
I don't mean the man who bursts in from stage right
Like a ghost not looking right or left and puts his special card
Into a concealed door in the wall as if escaping from the wrong cocktail party
Or the curtain has gone up on the wrong play.
I mean the ones who are not here.
The ones who are writing poems in the Mexican Gulf, for me.
My social life is in the bank.
In the queue that organises space and time
I feel things moving out of sight
And I have my place in the unhurried order of things.
All I have to do is stand in the queue. The girl at the desk says
What is the date your father died?
And when I tell her she pauses and says Lovely
And we are standing together in the rain seeing the lichen
On a grave in the Arran Islands.
In a minute she's going to ask me the name of my first dog.
I hold it ready in the mind.

A Smaller Variety of Wales

JOHN GALLAS

1
The sun is a counter of coal
cut thin, laid out,
and wet with light.

2
A fish with slate eyes
waits against cold water,
swimming to be still.

3
Brother Thomas
hunkers in heavy thought:
a bald hill wrapped in pines.

4
Howel Rees
lies in the
dead grey stones,
broken with no pain
by the blunt heads
of bursting bulbs.

5
The Giant sits
on his crater.
His arse is wet.
Big head in the rain.
He watches me pedal by,
a tangly meal.
I escape
in a small thunder.

6
When the Giant
was away
I climbed to the top
and the rim,
black-water-shod
in the wind,
where he had left
a long fart of mist in his seat
like a cold cushion,
to wait his return.

7
The Knights Hospitaller
of Ybsyty Ystwyth
are waiting to be kind.
They are early up,
brushed and blessed.
Their hands haunt
the dim road.
But it has rained for eternity,
and all the Walking-Faithful
are drowned
in fact, or in love.

8
One of the Several
King's Swords
lies hereabouts.
I saw it in an antibiotic fit,
two feet down
in a sludge of oakleaves
and a needle of light
bored by an ant
gilding the hilt, where it says,
Arthur Had Me Made.

9
Freewheeling down to Towyn
I heard a velvet bellow thrum the valley.
I looked around.
The fields were simply sheep.
And so I knew the cow was in the hill.
Was it an organ-hymn
of Heaven found, or
some trumpet-song
despaired from bones
that will not see the sun again.

10
Braich Goch Slate Quarry Workers Group Photograph 1890

I think I found the Bardo:
it's the one 4th row up
3rd from the left, beside
the pale, avoiding child:

ungroupishly of height,
Biblically white
of jacket, buttons, beard and westkit
and a billycock hat,

looming luminous between
the old dissolvement of a half-completed
blur, and coming back in colour
in a baseball cap.

Into the Blue

IAIN BAMFORTH

'J'écartai du ciel l'azur, qui est du noir...'
– Arthur Rimbaud, 'Delirium'

WANDERING AROUND the Musée d'art et d'histoire on a visit to the Swiss city of Neuchâtel, I stopped for a while in front of the monumental painting *Effet de soleil sur les Hautes Alpes du Valais en face de la chaîne du Mont-Rose*, 1843–44. It was the work of Alexandre Calame (1810–64), a Swiss painter who made Alpine scenes his calling card. White-capped mountains formed an extended backdrop to a range of bare brown slopes guarding an untroubled turquoise lake, the entire upper half of the painting being given over to a clear blue sky depicted in subtle gradations of that colour. It was the sky rather than the barren scene of rocks and mountains which caught my eye, and the empirically informed way in which Calame had rendered its nuances as the *bleu bleuet* became powdery and then deepened into ultramarine and cyan above the range of snow-covered peaks in the distance.

What the German poet and mining engineer Novalis called 'atmosphereology' had matured by the nineteenth century into meteorology – a new science that caught the public imagination. Every new science comes with its own instruments, and one that was popular in Calame's day was the cyanometer. It was an invaluable device for landscape artists too. This simple handheld analogue instrument registers the intensity of blueness of the atmosphere. It had been developed a generation before by the remarkable eighteenth-century Swiss geologist and inventor Horace-Bénédict de Saussure, and became well-known enough for Lord Byron to lampoon it in *Don Juan* as an instrument for measuring the blueness of 'bluestockings' – the name of an independent and educated women's movement in eighteenth-century England.

Saussure's circular cyanometer had fifty-two shades from white ('zero degrees') to black ('fifty-one degrees') to measure the blue of the sky, which Saussure believed was due to the agency of moist particles in the air. Saussure, who is generally credited as being the first Alpinist, was enraptured by the distinctive blue of the sky above the Swiss mountains: it held 'in its grandeur and its dazzling purity, an element of death and infinite sadness'.

Intense blue – the blue of lapis, Egyptian blue (a copper pigment known to the Romans as *caeruleum*), even the glaucous blue of the goddess Athena – was always outside the ordinary. Like sacred things generally, blue could be dangerous to get too close to. In Derek Jarman's last film (and testament), a deep saturated blue not dissimilar to International Klein Blue – the deep ultramarine monochrome made famous by the visual artist Yves Klein who was otherwise famous for his 'leaps into the void' – fills the screen for seventy-nine minutes while a narrating voice describes Jarman's fear of enveloping blindness and impending death. This, we intuit, is all the transcendence the filmmaker anticipates in the time left to him as he moves beyond the 'pandemonium of image' into Universal Blue. It will not be the theophanic blue of Fra Angelico.

On 20 June 1802, during their extended tour of middle America, Cuba and what was then called New Granada, Humboldt and his French botanist companion Aimé Bonpland set off in frock coats and walking shoes to attempt an ascent of Chimborazo, the daunting glacier-decked summit at the end of the Ecuadorian Volcanic Arc, at that time thought to be the highest mountain in the world. An oil painting by Friedrich Georg Weitsch shows them standing together with Indian guides and mules on a bare stretch of the altiplano at 4,000 metres with an impressive view of the snow-capped summit a farther 2,300 metres above them. They were prevented from scaling the summit by an impassable ice-wall and their lack of proper climbing equipment: nobody at that time had ever scaled such heights. Contemplating the view at 4,000 metres, they were testimony to Burke's notion of the sublime: that it required the spectator to climb mountains and not just admire them. Both men look composed and collected, when in truth they had been having difficulty breathing and were suffering some of the other effects of high altitude (nausea and vertigo). But Humboldt took out his cyanometer, and recorded the degree of blueness on Saussure's scale. It was forty-six degrees, the darkest blue ever seen – twice the value that would typically be measured at midday on a cloudless day in the Mediterranean.

Though the cyanometer could measure the degree of blueness, there was still much speculation about *why* the sky should be blue at all. It was after all a question that had been tormenting philosophers, poets and small children since the beginnings of recorded history – an apparently naive question. It is one as vast as the world itself. Giambattisto Vico in his influential work of speculative philosophy *Scienza Nuova* (1725) claimed that pondering the sky was the primal event in human consciousness. It is certainly true that a blue sky stirs even avowedly godless imaginations. Relating the exaltation he felt getting up before dawn in Toulon to sit at his bay window, the French historian Jules Michelet wrote about the steely clarity of the air when he could see (like a god) for miles into the distance. 'An intangible shade of blue – a blue the rosy dawn as yet respected and did not dare disturb, a holy ether, a sublimated spirit – made all Nature spiritual.'

Even the title of Ludwig Teick's *Das alte Buch, oder die Reise ins Blaue hinein* (1834) offers a sally into the wild blue yonder, the German expression for an enterprise undertaken without an aim in mind. The only limit is a blue one. 'I have been doing some skying', as John Constable told a friend. Constable, one of its great painters, always paid special attention to aerial phenomena and the effect of light on landscape, repudiating the 'white sheet' technique in landscape painting that made the sky a neutral background against which objects stood in relief: 'Clouds moving very fast with occasional very bright openings on the blue', is scribbled on the back of one of his sky studies. He had been inspired by the cloud studies of Luke Howard, whose famous 1803 'Essay on the Modifications of Clouds' established the Latinate taxonomy still used today for their 'production, suspension and destruction'. Constable was being faithful to the medium Aristotle had called the 'transparent' (*diaphonos*) more than two thousand years beforehand. Ruskin told his students to make a careful study of the sky: its pure blue was not just a hue 'but rather a profound, vibrating and transparent body of penetrating air.' If a sense of cosmic harmony had evaporated, it been replaced by nature as a kind of half-understood hermeneutics that needed deciphering, as in 'Tintern Abbey', where Wordsworth speaks of 'A presence that disturbs [him] with the joy / Of elevated thoughts; a sense sublime' dwelling in the ocean and the air and 'the blue sky, and the mind of man'.

Leonardo da Vinci had spent months drafting a book in which he recapitulated those two thousand years of thinking about why the sky is blue and enlarged them with his own insightful remarks. Centuries before Calame, he reached the conclusion that 'the blue air makes distant mountains appear blue', and applied this heuristic to his own landscape painting: a subtle admixture of blues allowed him to create an illusion of distance and objects set back from the foreground. (The most impressive works of classical Chinese painting are also devoted to rendering remoteness through moisture-laden air and the effects of precipitation.) As for a scientific explanation, Leonardo believed that 'minute, imperceptible particles' were attracted by solar rays which then 'seem luminous against the deep, intense darkness of the region of fire that forms a covering above them', which is not far removed from Aristotle's explanation in *On the Senses*. Leonardo even tried to capture an 'artificial sky' in a bottle, something Saussure tried to do in his time too, using a saturated solution of copper sulphate and ammonia.

In the decade of Calame's death, the physicist John Tyndall – also a keen Alpinist – thought he had found the secret of the everlasting blue, and called his agent 'aequeous vapour'. He mixed the sky in a bottle too, and was able to confect a mixture of hydrochloric acid vapour and air that appeared blue in white light. Even Ruskin, who had little time for science, was impressed: he thought that producing a perfect blue in a tube '[was] magic of the finest sort'. This is now known as the Tyndall effect. Tyndall held to the idea that particles in the air create the blueness of blue sky, but Ruskin's suspicion that molecules in the air actually scatter the rays of the sun's light differently according to wavelength was closer to the mark. It was a hunch confirmed by Einstein's paper on opalescence in 1910, which showed this scattering effect in detail, and incidentally confirmed the reality of atoms. Revealing that the colour of the sky is caused by gas molecules scattering the sun's light had led to a convincing piece of circumstantial evidence in favour of atomic theory. 'The sky cannot be blue if atoms are not real', as Paul Pesic points out in his book, *Sky in a Bottle*.

Sometimes we associate the blueness of the sky with the azure of the sea. 'This indefinite lucid blue pallor of the aquatic evening' as the Portuguese poet Pessoa put it (writing as Bernardo Soares) in his *The Book of Disquiet*. And then we feel as if we're drowning.

Almost contemporaneously with Pessoa, Robert Musil gave expression to the overpowering sense of vertigo that affects his wayward adolescent protagonist in his 1906 novel *The Confusion of Young Törless*. The eponymous hero goes for a walk in the park and, lying in the grass, notices 'as if for the first time' a bottomless blue gap between scuds of cloud in the vault of the autumn sky. He is seized by anguish – by a blue funk. 'He felt it must be possible if only he had a long, long ladder, to climb up and into it. But the farther he penetrated, lifting himself up as he raised his eyes, the deeper the blue luminous background receded.' Infinity, which had seemed to young Törless a concept that had been thoroughly tamed and domesticated – and had even been made to do 'circus tricks' in his mathematics classes – had suddenly broken loose and gone on the rampage. His abyssal vision was the same one which Vico thought must have struck the 'giants' – Noah's descendants – who roamed the densely wooded earth after the Flood and turned their gaze to the prospect of the sky where the deity insisted on speaking in signs. It is also a precise enactment of Friedrich von Schlegel's definition of *Sehnsucht*, that 'vague feeling of deepest longing' which knows no limits, but rather 'climbing step by step, never ceases to rise further' (*Philosophy of Language and the Word*, 1829).

Törless hadn't found the ultimate lair of blueness. In 1934, the American naturalist and pioneering ecologist William Beebe described his descent off the coast of Nonsuch Island in the Bermudas with the inventor of the bathysphere Otis Barton to a record three thousand feet below sea level. As the steel sphere of this cramped, creaking construction with its tiny porthole was winched into the deep, and the warm reassuring red glow of the terrestrial day disappeared, giving way to 'chill and night and death', he tried to describe what was left, a twilight shade that was paradoxically phosphorescent: 'It was of an indefinable translucent blue quite unlike anything I have ever seen in the upper world, and it excited our optic nerves in a most confusing manner [...] the blueness of the blue, both outside and inside our sphere, seemed to pass materially through the eye into our very beings.' It was only by shutting his eyes and opening them again that he could register 'the terrible slowness of the change from dark blue to blacker blue'.

Beebe was describing the cyanotic chill of subaqueous blue. Midnight blue. There was no way to verify whether that deepest blue emanated from the absolute zone of Saussure's degree 51, or whether it was a kind of dark light phenomenon generated by his own eyes. Depth is just depth, a dimension where nothing ever comes to light. Nonetheless, in the confines of a tiny bathysphere, cramped and in mortal danger, it seems he had an intense experience of what Pythagoras knew as 'the unlimited'.

There we have it: those who survive the urge to go to the ends of the earth often come back with a pressing need to tell us about the cornflower beauty of what can be observed in daylight hours, under normal atmospheric pressure, and at sea level.

Three Poems

Nina Bogin

Pink

It was her favorite colour.
In the small, overheated bathroom,
pink bath rug, pink towels, pink
shower curtain, pink toilet paper...
Even now I can feel the warmth
hissing through the coils of the radiator
as I washed my hands surrounded
by pink and felt as if I might choke
if I stayed one more minute
in that narrow space –
Grandma Sophie's tiny haven
of comfort, her pastel dream
of a life without torment.
She asked for so little, only
for everyone to be happy,
or short of that, then simply
to be allowed to wish
that everyone should be happy,
as if happiness were something
that might possibly exist...
On that last visit to the apartment –
she was already ill, shrunken
in her pink bathrobe –
she followed us, my father
and me, out into the hallway
that smelled, year in, year out,
of homemade chicken soup,
and hugged me tight
whispering fiercely
into my chest
I love you I love you I love you I love you

Practical Joke

Hard to imagine
my father's father
whom I never knew
going into a corner shop
in 1934 or 1935
and saying 'I'll take
two of those' –
celluloid turds
he'd place on
the back seat of the car
before the ladies –
dressed for an outing,
his sister-in-law and wife –
got in. Oh
their shrieks!
Rubber spiders,
wind-up mice –
bellyfuls of laughs!
He looks out
from a photo in sepia.
Under a perky fedora,
his apologetic, schoolboy grin.

Sleepless

4 a.m. Sounds come in single file:
one ring of the telephone,
one tap on the roof,
one bark of a deer in the woods.
How I wish it would bark again!
And that I could dream
its animal sleep
on a bed of leaves
along the stream...
Happiness has fled.
Why does it make such a difference?
Come on, take yourself in hand
and make a shopping list instead:
string to tie up the tomato plants,
a paring knife, matches, a pen,
candles and storm lamps
for the times ahead.

Flagrant Stamen (Voyager)

NED DENNY

The little Love-god lying once asleep...

Let me beam you a song that is the song
of you all, a true story of a cruise as long
as its horror is real and which I still endure,
the red blink of my heart the one thing sure
in this utter ocean as black as it is ice;
of this freight of golden howls, the frail device
of my face parting the tides of the sun
on the endless night-watch, the towering
cliffs of birdless islands revolving past my wing
and my tin feet bathed in the absolute zero
of their wake, an automatic sorrow
running through the circuits of my sea-eaten brain.
The man still inside the blessings of the rain –
fine earth underfoot, a daughter or son

trailing behind and then darting ahead –
cannot conceive of those currents I've rode, those dead
winter surges of my shaken trajectory,
the frost that patterns me like a story
chiselled on the tomb of a navigating king;
and nothing to hear but the void pulsating,
the vacant whirr, the ringed orb's subtle drone,
an iron silence in which no gull praised
branching wave and branching light, no curlew amazed
the humming mind awake with its ghost of a cry
(but I have their records stored like wines, I
guard their lyrics like the dead's delighted laughter),
not one note perched on that echoed hall's rafter
where I sailed on through its mansions of bone.

What I did hear, in the permanent roar
of the standing hexagon on Saturn's north shore,
was a shriek as of a wraith with metal feathers
nitrogen-dewed, vast inclement weathers
radiating outwards like haze that taints the sky;
but none to share the vision, no hand close by
with that shining ratio love unfolds
or its sweet kinship of divine disdain,
far as I was from you who have to dose the pain
of crowded solitude by tricking out your cells
with mimic love and light (those broadcast spells,
intoxicants all); alone I trace the dark,
the paths of night, no companionable ark
but the sole witness of what my craft beholds

on the bleak streets of this high sea. Shadows
lose substance as the sun recedes, iced methane snows
on Titan, down the unavailing space grit rains
like someone is sowing porcelain grains;
my dials tremble with an exile's vertigo,
quake between joy and terror, wild to go
with the towering stream of the central tree
that waves like an ash on a day of storm,
to be sucked along those entwined boughs to the warm
airs and opening worlds of a bird-minded race
(just as no man's so at home in his face,
so deep in the arms of his darling one

that he does not sweat at the thought of the One
and his lonely flight to the Alone, the mystery,

that he's never struck by music's silence
or the blank in the gaze of so-called science
or the immateriality of that and this
or the absence in the depth of a kiss,
conceiving instead a thirst for the furthest shore).
I think of your ascendant woods lit once more,
of leafing spires in the vague city's maze
and a bright green spire where mantises pray;
I think of those whose minds will discover the way
to the land's brink, that tangled footpath to the stars
you climb with closed eyes through the sky's briars,
the returning track of which the sure bird sings
when its plain song summons inexpressible things
perched on the border of your nights and days.

Such ones will seem odd to all whose sense
of what is and isn't real is hijacked by events
narrated on the airwaves, each new fearfest
drumming home the point that home's where you're safest;
in the room's corner, where a live fire should inform,
a digital flicker keeps nobody warm.
But now my warbling heart (*wirbil*, 'whirlwind')
spins beyond its case to remotely view
that open prison I have left, the whale-psalmed blue,
the great curving routes of the migratory spheres
and the turbulence of their atmospheres,
then comes back with a vast screech of admonition:
forget your readings and forget your mission,
keep on and don't look back until you find

joys holier than that pen where life means death
can give you, that paradise where a dragon's breath
rusts the fruit on the branch and the coin in your hand,
that demon-sucked and pestilential land
where disease is a business and health is a loss,
where youth is bent, where a sword can reach across
a hemisphere to gut an ambling man
and sharp-eyed spears drift at the edge of space;
and, truly, a warrior who would gain his place
amongst the angels, they who sing the raging calm,
must take his stand against the ring-fenced farm –
if he cares to fight for the living epitaph
of his great-great-granddaughter's unenslaved laugh –
where the meat and milk and blood is human.

The sunlight is veiled, the empires it grew
looted and labelled, the king's jewelled retinue
scattered, his exploits a stele that none can translate;
and no gold to give that is not gold plate,
no exulting heroes but smooth-voiced snakes in suits
('strategic consultants', the mind that computes)
who blanch beneath a diplomatic smile;
and the letters of Nature's sacred book
unillumined in the eyes of those too dazed to look,

the drained men a premature senility
curls up like leaves; and in that grey city,
behind a brace of code-locked doors, a lord who trusts
in his wealth – Selah – yet secretly lusts
for a body that death might never defile

grows pale at the thought of his failing strength
and all those proud forebears tuned to the grave's wavelength,
for a name's not a house that the storm won't lay bare
and you can't buy grace with a silver prayer –
hear me open my dark saying – and piles of gold
won't make that strange chamber one degree less cold,
recalling the wages of monstrous greed.
Wondrous the one who flows in His stillness,
embodies the bedrock, whose breath is the clearness
of the world-spangled heavens and the lichened wood,
and blessed are those who live simply – not 'good',
but listening less to the talk than the thunder –
and lost is the herd with no sense of wonder
(he who thinks he knows is a fool indeed,

not once having died while still drawing breath:
'Almighty God, what is this? My boy, this is death').
To recognise the Word which glows in every stone
is to feel your flesh grow light, is to own

nothing but that wild and tender sense of creaturehood,
is to step gently, it being understood
that the way is a way of restraint;
an outer and an inner cleanliness
becomes the pupil – Hugiaine! – who judges less
than he suffers with all those who moan in their sleep,
clear in enmity as he is in deep
love, casting no man in the hieroglyphic fire
before his time, knowing His code is higher
and wider than conception can paint

or poem build. Let no soul succumb
to deceit but consider what it has become
and what it is, a child of the star-toned origin
all things point to and where they rebegin,
and why and how it is obstructed from seeing
that radiance that is the body's being,
the birthright of whole-eyed women and men
upright on the earth. Praise to the One
and to the Holy Mother Spirit and the Son,
Christos and Sophia – words that believe in silence
and She who is the light of that immense
and waking garden – and courage to the fool
who holds the flagrant stamen these waters cannot cool,
now and forever. Onwards. Amen.

Talking to a Nanny Goat

Umberto Saba revisited

PATRICK WORSNIP

Alive I spoke to a nation of the dead.
Dead I refuse laurel and ask oblivion.

THAT SEEMS AN ODD EPITAPH for a poet to write on himself after a lifetime seeking greater public acclaim and receiving it in his final years. But then, Umberto Saba, who was born in Trieste in 1883 and died in nearby Gorizia in 1957, and who is now considered one of the three greatest Italian poets of the twentieth century (along with Eugenio Montale and Giuseppe Ungaretti), was in many ways an odd man.

Take that surname. The writer (he also composed short stories and an unfinished novel) was born Umberto Poli to a Jewish mother and a father who, though born a Roman Catholic, had converted to Judaism in order to marry her, making Umberto, by Jewish reckoning, a full Jew. But from the start of his literary activities he experimented with pseudonyms – admittedly not an uncommon practice at that or other times. These included Umberto da Montereale (the town his father's family came from), Umberto Lopi (an anagram of Poli) and even Chopin. But the one he settled on, and eventually officially changed his name to, was Saba.

Academics have long debated what it means and why he chose it. Theories have come and gone, including that it is a Hebrew word for 'bread' or was somehow linked with his beloved wet-nurse, a Slovenian Catholic named Josefa Gabrovic. The one thing that seems certain is that he borrowed it, with permission, from a fellow Triestine Jew, Giorgio Fano, who had also adopted it for unknown reasons and who became known as an idealist philosopher and expert on Benedetto Croce. I have no Hebrew but the *Jewish Encyclopedia* says that 'saba' is a Talmudic term meaning not bread but 'an old man'. In the latest discussion I have seen (2012), Saba critic Fulvio Senardi says Umberto 'could hardly have been unaware' of this meaning and would have thought it appropriate for someone whose maternal great-grandfather was a celebrated Biblical scholar. Saba is also the Italian for Sheba (as in Queen of). I end up by asking another Saba expert, Elvio Guagnini, an emeritus professor of Trieste University, why there appears to be no record of anyone having asked the poet about the name. 'Maybe they did and maybe he replied in an evasive manner,' he says.

In this series of occasional articles on poets in Italy I have stressed their ties to the places where they were born or lived. Of no one is this truer than of Saba, who spent much of his life in Trieste and wrote frequently about it, including in a book of poems entitled *Trieste and a Woman* (1912 – the woman was his wife, Lina, of whom more later).

The city lies at the top right-hand corner of the Adriatic Sea, at the end of a narrow tongue of coastal land jutting into Slovenia. At the junction of the

Slavic, Germanic and Mediterranean worlds, it has the kind of complicated history you would expect. Though majority Italian-speaking, it belonged for centuries to the Austro-Hungarian Habsburg empire, providing it with a valuable seaport. The blue waters that figure in many Saba poems are not just beautiful, they are Trieste's commercial lifeblood. In 1912, at Duino Castle a few miles along the coast, the Austrian poet Rainer Maria Rilke was embarking on his *Duino Elegies* – so unlike Saba's work it is hard to believe the two men were aware of each other. Trieste passed to Italy after World War I, but came under effective German control after the fall of Fascism in World War II, as did other parts of northern Italy where the Allies had not yet arrived. When that conflict ended, Tito's Yugoslav partisans took over the city and a number of their political opponents disappeared, never to be seen again. But after just over a month it came under British-US administration until 1954, when it reverted to Italy, whose rule was finally ratified by the Treaty of Osimo in 1975. To this day, some fine Austrian architecture perpetuates the memory of the Habsburgs.

Saba stressed the isolated position of Trieste on the fringes of Italian culture. To be born there in 1883 was like being born elsewhere in 1850, he wrote, describing himself as 'peripheral' and 'backward'. That judgment perhaps undervalues a city that was also the birthplace of the novelist Italo Svevo, author of *The Conscience of Zeno*, and the on-off residence of James Joyce from 1905 to 1915. Today you can follow Saba, Svevo and Joyce 'itineraries' in Trieste – essentially a series of plaques on buildings associated with them.

Saba was born in the Jewish ghetto, which was to be demolished, along with much of the Old City, in a redevelopment plan in the 1930s. His father had already left the family home and his mother, who denounced her husband as a 'murderer', had Umberto fostered by Gabrovic for his first three years, later sending him for extended periods to relatives in Padua. Despite little higher education he had begun to write both poetry and prose by the time he was twenty. In 1909 he married Carolina (Lina) Wölfler, also Jewish, in a synagogue at the bottom of the steep Via del Monte. It no longer exists (there's one elsewhere in Trieste) but when I visit I find that next door is a well-appointed Jewish museum that gives full details of the Jewish community that was so important in Saba's life.

There had been Jews in Trieste since the Middle Ages, but they increased after the city became a free port in the eighteenth century, reaching more than five thousand, a figure exceeded only by Rome and Milan. Most of them were not particularly observant but hung together as a community, playing a disproportionate role in business and cultural life. Many of Saba's friends were Jewish, as was the psychoanalyst he went to after developing a neurotic condition in later life – Edoardo Weiss, who had studied with Freud in Vienna and brought the master's techniques to Italy. With a family background like his, Saba was a prime case for them.

Despite his alliance with Hitler, Italy's Fascist dictator Benito Mussolini only made serious moves against the Jews in 1938, passing racial laws that deprived them of various civil rights. Even then, it was anti-semitism Italian-style, not German-style, according to Saba's biographer, the late Stelio Mattioni. The laws had 'so many holes and escape clauses and such broad generalisations that they allowed all sorts of exemptions and did not legitimise Jews being hunted down, segregated or eliminated as a pollutant of the Aryan race,' Mattioni says in his *History of Umberto Saba*. Saba applied successfully to be exempted from them on grounds of his cultural services to the state. But, like some other Jews, he officially withdrew from the Jewish community. He remained untroubled until the German takeover in 1943, when he was plunged into extreme danger. The Nazis were not going to be impressed by his exemption, his poetry or his mixed parentage. He fled with his family to Florence, also unliberated by the Allies but easier to hide in. The Sabas evaded capture by moving from one apartment to another, their helpers including the non-Jewish Montale – at no little danger to himself.

Saba ended up at odds with Judaism, at least in its religious aspect. In a 1949 letter to the psychiatrist Joachim Flescher that was not meant to be published, he denounced 'old men crushed flat by their sense of guilt, reciting a chorus of prayers to the Almighty in a dead language that none of them understands'. While having nothing against Jews in general, he said, he would 'shoot in the back all those who practise circumcision'. And yet a famous 1910 poem, 'The Nanny Goat', has been taken as voicing the tragedies of the Jewish people. Here it is (the translation is mine):

I spoke to a nanny goat.
She was by herself in the meadow, on a chain.
Stuffed full of grass, the rain
soaking her, she bleated.

That steady bleating chimed
with my sorrow. And I answered, first in jest,
then because sorrow lingers for all time,
has one voice, does not change. The moan
of this voice I heard then
in a nanny goat left on her own.

And I heard lamenting
in a goat with a semitic face
every other wrong, every other living thing.

Saba wrote later, disingenuously or not, that the poem had been misinterpreted, that the description of the goat's face was 'predominantly visual' and that when he composed it he had 'no conscious thought either for or against the Jews'.

That aspect aside, it is clear from 'The Nanny Goat' that we are dealing with a *sui generis* poet far from any 'isms' of the time. Like Guido Gozzano (who was born in the same year but died in 1916), he was initially influenced by Gabriele D'Annunzio, whom he visited in 1907 at a luxury rented villa on the Tuscan coast. D'Annunzio, a man not noted for his modesty, said after hearing Saba read some of his verses: 'I am the greatest Italian poet, but it's not ruled out that you will be one of the most important.' The fixation did not last long. Four years later Saba wrote a manifesto, 'What Remains for Poets to Do' – which was, he said, to make their poetry truthfully reflect their experience.

He compared poems by Alessandro Manzoni (more familiar for his novel *The Betrothed*) to what he admitted was better work by D'Annunzio, preferring the former for never saying 'a word that does not correspond perfectly to his vision' while the latter 'exaggerates or entirely fakes passions and admirations alien to his temperament'. Saba sent his article to the fashionable literary magazine *La Voce*, which rejected it. It remained unpublished until after his death.

Saba cast himself as a mainstream Italian poet, writing in classical Italian forms, in a tradition stretching from Dante through Leopardi. He entitled his collection *Il Canzoniere* (The Songbook), a deliberate re-use of Petrarch's term in the fourteenth century. In the literary ferment of the early twentieth century, reacting against the poetic icons of the recent past, this was not what critics wanted, and it's easy to see why *La Voce* would have disapproved of Saba's moralising tone. But Saba would have no truck with movements like Futurism and Hermeticism (though Montale was a lifelong friend) and also reacted angrily when grouped with the Crepusculars, headed by Gozzano. His insistence that poetry should be both lucid and autobiographical (he categorised the *Canzoniere* as a sort of historical novel about himself) did not immediately play well either. Abroad, too, there's little doubt that Montale, with his complex thought, punchy imagery and sinuous free verse, has travelled better than Saba, whose mastery of the hendecasyllable (roughly equivalent to the English iambic pentameter) is lost on most non-Italian readers. And Saba's direct expression of his feelings will seem to some to teeter on the brink of sentimentality. I know of no critical book in English devoted entirely to him, the best analysis being in Joseph Cary's *Three Modern Italian Poets* (second edition 1993 – the other two are Montale and Ungaretti).

Saba was obsessed for much of his life with what he saw as the literary world's failure to understand or appreciate him. He even took the unusual step of writing a commentary on his own work, *History and Chronology of the* Canzoniere, in which he employed yet another pseudonym and wrote of himself in the third person. But things have gradually changed, at least in Italy. The critic Giovanni Titta Rosa said Saba's poetry (the final edition of the *Canzoniere* ran to six hundred pages written over half a century, while a collected poems published after his death adds nearly two hundred pieces that he excluded) 'has accompanied our generation like a friendly voice'. Ask anyone in football-mad Italy who reads any poetry at all which of Saba's poems they like best and they'll probably tell you it's 'Goal' (the English word is used), which describes the agony of a goalkeeper who has just let in a shot, as his counterpart at the far end exults.

To what extent, though, is Saba a modern poet, given his scorn for many of the trappings of modernism? To seek an answer to this question is one of my aims in visiting Trieste, whose former cosmopolitanism is perhaps echoed now mainly by the heavy trucks, bearing licence plates of every country between here and Russia, that thunder past on the motorway through the hills above the city.

I contact Elvio Guagnini and ask him to meet me in a café that Saba used to frequent and was once known as the Municipio, later the Garibaldi. It's now called the Piazza Grande, the former name of the huge Unification of Italy Square, as it's now known. Still with me? It was reportedly here that Saba wrote one of my favourite poems, 'Winter Noon', which recounts how, looking out of the window, he sees a toy balloon sail high across the clear, cold sky and pictures the anguish of the child who has lost it. Elvio tells me the café has moved a few yards from its former location in the *municipio* (city hall) itself next door. He also warns me that if you order a cappuccino in Trieste you'll get what elsewhere is called a *caffè macchiato*. To be served the conventional article, you need to ask for a *cappuccino italiano*. (Trieste, where illycaffè was founded, remains a coffee city.) Turning to Saba, Elvio confirms that his reputation has steadily gained. 'The more time has passed, the more justice has been done to him,' he says. 'Saba has a modernity of his own, but it's not that of the Hermetics.' Its source, he adds, lies in his 'disquiet'. Elsewhere, he has written: 'Saba's modernity is due to his extreme sensitivity to the complexity that results from the contradictions of human existence.'

My true Mecca in Trieste, though, is the Umberto Saba Antiquarian Bookshop, a few streets away. It used to belong to the poet, who bought it in 1919, and served as his main source of income throughout his life. In 1939, to be on the safe side, he nominally handed it over to his Christian business partner Carlo Cerne but resumed control after the war. After Saba died, Carlo again ran it until his own death in 1981, when it passed to his son Mario, who still owns it. For good measure, it's on the site of a building where Joyce had lived with his companion Nora Barnacle, and where their son Giorgio was born in 1905.

Inside, it's everybody's idea of a second-hand bookshop – dark and cavernous with shelves from floor to ceiling stacked with books of varying epochs and states of repair. Mario greets me. Now seventy-five, he can remember the poet. 'Saba was a difficult person,' he recalls. 'When clients came, they preferred to talk to my father.' As it happens, a client comes in as we are talking and Mario introduces him, saying he's ninety-two and that his greatest claim to fame is that he was once goalkeeper for Triestina, the city's premier football club. Later, I ask if he's the man who figures in 'Goal'. 'No,' Mario says. 'He's too young.' (A quick calculation shows he would have been about ten or twelve at the time). I ask about the future of the shop. Mario peers at me through his owlish spectacles. He'd like to retire, but the only person he could hand over to is his daughter and she lives in London. Business has been hit by the internet. 'You saw I have a client who's ninety-two,' he says. 'I've got another who's ninety-three. The new generation is not interested in anything. Go to a furniture store, go to IKEA – how many bookcases are there?' The ideal solution for him would be to turn the shop into a Saba Museum. There's long been talk of such a project, but in today's Italy funding is scarce. I leave and inspect a bronze statue of Saba placed at a nearby corner. It's based on a splendid photo of the poet kept in the shop showing him striding down a street, but omits his characteristic pipe (when he died at a Gorizia care home he was found with pipe and matches still clutched in his outstretched hand). That could be about all there's going to be in the way of a museum.

As sometimes happens with famous writers, Saba had an awkward relationship with his home town. Having once had a passing acquaintance with Mussolini, who visited his shop in 1921, a year before taking power in Rome, he tended to the left after World War II, denouncing the rise of the Christian Democrats as 'after the black Fascist the black priest'. But Mattioni says it is 'simply absurd' to call him a political man. Once asked to what political party he belonged, he replied: 'To the psychoanalyst party.' In early 1948, however, he published a newspaper article, 'If I were named governor of Trieste', saying he would like to pass a law condemning to the firing squad anyone inciting racial hatred between Italians and Slavs. A worthy sentiment, perhaps, but one that went down badly in a city whose political future was in the balance, with rule by Yugoslavia still a possibility.

Controversy also lingers over his private, or not so private, life. His marriage to Lina was stormy, even though it lasted forty-seven years until Lina died nine months before Umberto, and they were in some ways very tied to each other. Soon after they wed, Lina announced, to Umberto's dismay, that she was pregnant and gave birth in 1910 to their daughter Linuccia. Upset by her husband's negative reaction to the baby, Lina walked out the following year and took up with a local painter. But the following year they were back together, perhaps under pressure from Lina's family. Lina, for her part, was less than thrilled by his poem of that period 'To My Wife' (now hailed as a masterpiece), in which he compares her successively to a hen, a heifer, a dog, a rabbit, a swallow and an ant.

In the early 1920s, Saba employed a series of young women as assistants in his shop and they too appear, with changed names, in poems of a very different sort. Did he have affairs with them? It's hard to say. But that he fancied them he scarcely bothers to conceal. We know from a memoir by her son that one, Giulia Morpurgo, whom Saba calls Chiaretta, left because of his advances (he gave her a glowing reference for her next employer). Lina, unable perhaps to take the moral high-ground, took a relaxed view according to Mattioni, saying that when Umberto was *innamorato* at least she was left in peace. You don't have to be politically correct to find the poems about these *fanciulle* (girls) patronising and sexist; writers win few admirers these days by saying, as Saba does in the punch-line of one about a woman he calls Paolina, that 'all she had was her *cosetta*' (literally 'little thing', the euphemism somehow even more off-putting than the sentiment). We don't expect poets necessarily to have opinions we agree with (think of Ezra Pound) or to be people we would choose to sit next to at a dinner party; we just want them to write great poems. And fortunately Saba could do much better than this. For me, his greatest quality is his ability to universalise the humblest image or passing feeling.

Readers today will doubtless look with more sympathy than during Saba's lifetime at his homoerotic side. Late in life he wrote part of a novel, *Ernesto*, which has some claim to be Italy's equivalent of E. M. Forster's *Maurice* and was likewise published only after its author's death. Saba's book recounts the homosexual, as well as the heterosexual, initiation of a sixteen-year-old boy in turn-of-the-century Trieste. Was the same-sex encounter based on some experience Saba had with a co-worker while briefly employed in his teens by a flour merchant? Mattioni doubts it and quotes the openly gay poet Sandro Penna as denying that Saba was also gay. Not everyone is convinced, though, and there is no question that he became more than casually interested in a good-looking young Triestine, Federico Almansi, some forty years his junior, who showed early promise as a poet but started to develop schizophrenia when he was twenty-five, eventually to die in an institution.

My attempt to uncover what became of Saba's family leads into still more tangled thickets. I can't say I wasn't warned since Mattioni, who published his biography in 1989 but researched much of it in the 1960s, quotes Giorgio Fano as telling him that 'little is known about Saba, but the less known the better'. In 1941, the poet's daughter Linuccia married Lionello Giorni, a Triestine painter and a Catholic, in what Mattioni speculates may have been a liaison of convenience to protect her from racial persecution. The marriage, like Umberto's with Lina, endured, but after World War II Linuccia began a thirty-year relationship with Carlo Levi, author of the highly successful memoir *Christ Stopped at Eboli* and a noteworthy artist whose portrait of Saba in his favourite black beret adorns the dust jacket of my copy of the *Canzoniere*. She died in 1980 and I am told in Trieste that the only surviving family member – and even then not a blood relative – is a woman named Raffaella Acetoso, who lives in Rome. Raffaella is unable to see me but agrees to speak on the telephone. She says she is the daughter of Linuccia's husband, and I will leave that phraseology as it stands. She declines to identify her mother, except to say that it was not Linuccia, who 'did not love me'. And the name Acetoso? It's 'the surname of my mother's husband'. Reader, go figure. At all events, Raffaella ended up as the legal heir of both Saba and Levi. She tells me she believes Saba was bisexual but that 'Lina was the great love of his life'. Although a restorer of Venetian villas by profession, she has edited a volume of letters between Saba and Lina, but expresses despair about a decades-old plan to publish the poet's complete correspondence, a project the critic Senardi says is 'evidently on the rocks'. In Trieste, Elvio Guagnini told me that some owners of letters had refused to release them, but Raffaella blames the proposed publisher, Mondadori. Sixty years after Saba died, it seems, some of his letters remain sensitive.

Full-scale recognition for a world-class poet, albeit a curmudgeonly individual (some have said he was an old man – *saba*? – from his adolescence onwards), came late. Awarded three top Italian literary prizes – the Viareggio in 1946, the Lincei in 1950 and the Taormina in 1951 – he complained that he had to share the first with another writer and that the other two went up sharply in monetary value in subsequent years. When Trieste finally made its peace with him and held a ceremony in 1953 to mark his seventieth birthday, the poet, now ill and addicted to morphine, made a short speech and left, saying it was 'time for children of my age to go to bed'.

I end my quest for Saba in – where else? – the cemetery where he's buried in a grave with Lina and Linuccia. It's a Catholic cemetery where Svevo, who was born Jewish as Aron Ettore Schmitz but converted to Catholicism, is also buried. Italians don't like negative stuff on tombstones and the Sabas' does not contain the epitaph cited at the start of this article. Instead, quoting from one of his poems, it says he 'wept and understood for all'. I remember Elvio telling me that he was a lonely man, always looking through a window, observing the crowd but not part of it. In his poem 'The Suburb' he writes that he wanted 'to live the life / of all / to be like all / the men of all / days.' There's a story that the day he arrived in Salerno, south of Naples, in 1907 to start his military service, conscripts already there took him out to the cinema. Soldiers got in half-price, but Saba had not yet received his uniform. In one of the apparently few joyful moments in his life, his uniformed comrades told the cashier: 'Give him the discount, *he's one of us*' (my italics). In the vast cemetery on this hot August afternoon, it occurred to me that Saba was now at last 'like all the men of all days'.

Three Poems

RORY WATERMAN

Parable with Ageing Parent

They're both down by 9
    at table 5 – the

    bay window table! –
clicking cutlery

with the egg smells, clicks,
    scrapes and tiny talk,

    talking and scraping
at full Englishes.

The year dismantles
    against our wishes;

    he sees it over
her head, through warped glass:

dry leaves quave, pitch, or
    tousle ragged lawns.

    In here, buff lights burn,
the year dismantles,

and she pours coffee
    for herself, then him.

    There isn't enough.
Grains ride down the lip:

she doesn't see them,
    dark light is burning,

    the year dismantles.
'It's nice here!' she says

meaning something else
    it would hurt to say.

June Morning, Erewash Canal

The colliery's a country park:
    his old man shunted coal.
This young dad teaches his lad to fish
    at a bug-flecked winding hole
while opposite a brace of fish
    repeats between the reeds.
Like this, he bellows, hands on shoulders
    pulling the kid around,
who grimaces and squares his shoulders,
    wanting the world to know
he knows. May petals file across
    in fuddles of sun-dried snow.

Sleeper

You sat askew in a taxi, jolting past rush hour,
then took the sleeper home to watch your grandma –
her tight mouth sunk in shrunk surprise
still, though now her eyes were shut and breath,
not how she knew you, was all she'd battle for.

Bolting past coast then cornfields, through dusk then dark
you saw it all, then filled the flip-down berth.
And stitching your in-out sleep, the wheels battered on
sending their morse over towns, under trees, along cuttings.

Mansions in the Sky

The Rise and Fall of Branwell Brontë

SIMON ARMITAGE

William, It Was Really Nothing

The young pretender has cocked his hat
towards Westmorland. Picture the great bard,
mid-breakfast, letter in hand,
eyes on stalks and jaw hanging loose,
a loaded knife-blade of Dorothy's damson preserve
stalled between lidded porcelain jam-pot and toast,
blood-scabs of red sealing wax crumbed
on the cloud-white tablecloth.

(Thinks: if Paul Pogba cost eighty-nine million plus,
what am I worth?). Except

what glittered like charmed finches over Haworth Church
drifts as rain across Scafell Pike. No reply:
the parsonage clock patrols the night-shift
in jailors' boots. Outside the moors play dead.

Self Portrait

Allow me this moment
all to myself. Doctor,

there was no room to breathe
at the family gathering;

thin-skinned and out of kilter
I ducked behind

a thick stone pillar
then slipped outside

to Facebook and vape.
Doc, it was a no-brainer:

airbrush my own face
out of the picture

or photo-bomb
those darling ~~bitches witches~~ sisters

and moon there forever,
the eternal gooseberry.

So here's me having
a moment to myself,

clearing my head
as best I can,

all light and air, also known as
the nothing I am.

Initiation

It's leap year day
  eighteen-thirty-six
      when we lift the lid

on curtained rooms
  in the Three Graces Lodge
      to witness the scene:

how the novice is drawn
  from ante-chamber
      to inner sanctum

blindfolded, noosed.
  How his bared right arm
      and bared right leg

wear a downy haze
  of ginger hair.
      How he kneels,

bible in hand,
  knife and compass
      aligned to his breast,

to swear the secret
  of tokens and grips,
      and receives his tools –

the gavel and set-square
  and sinker of lead
      to keep him

centred and level, sober and sane.
  Then he wobbles home
      up the cobbled lane.

The Smallprint

i)
Simultaneously
and with both hands:
that's how well (they said) he could write.

ii)
Elf-words, pixie-talk,
the sub-atomic scribble
of imps and sprites.

iii)
Popular wisdom decrees
you can't fold a piece of paper
more than seven times.

iv)
At that age, to confuse signature
with autograph
would be a tell-tale sign.

v)
The word Robins-
on takes some spotting
with the naked eye;

vi)
(treasure hunters – it's
column two, just after halfway down,
right hand side).

vii)
The script-work's bacterial,
with antibiotics
still a hundred years down the line.

viii)
Pinch-points at the corners,
stresses and fraying along the creases
and rhymes.

ix)
The day comes
when every adult must
up their font-size.

x)
Right under his nose,
the reams and sheaves to which
the old man was blind.

xi)
Using the Rorschach test,
read into those watermarks
whatever you like.

xii)
Mostly at the holes now
is where we notice
the light.

Wallet

Man-purse, portion
    of heart, hank
            of man-heart,

the rolled heart-meat
    tethered
            with tongue-strap,

the hide weathered
    by hand-sweat,
            body heat.

Boned fillet
    of man-breast,
            flipped open it's

book-like,
    the heart-steak
            knifed into folds and layers,

the splayed leaves of flesh
    lying tooled
            and grained.

This pocket
    for banknotes, bills,
            this crevice

for love-letters, verse.
    Deeper in,
            a condom pouched

in its tinfoil wrap,
    the looped pencil holder
            holstering

a clean syringe,
    a dealer's number
            encoded, stowed

in a secret tier,
    credit cards
            maxed to the limit

and edged with coke,
    the prile
            of photo-booth snaps,

dead faces interred
    with a sprig of hair,
            clutched in the heart's heart.

Lost and Found

1) Lost
Stolen or unintentionally removed, one artist's daybook and journal, hand-stitched vellum bound in the choicest rhinoceros hide and fastened with white-gold buckle. Of incalculable creative value, said object comprises detailed ethnographic portrait studies, philosophical observations, intellectual meditations, Latin and Greek inscription, archaeological illustrations from the classical period, delicate line-drawings and original drafts of poetic works (including short formal lyrics and extracts from epic cycles) in the modern 'Romantic' style. Artefact immediately identifiable via its quality penmanship, mature quillwork and distinguished calligraphy. Owner an educated gentleman of forgiving heart; finder assured at least a footnote in the annals of British art and literature plus the gratitude of the nation. Reward: declared upon presentation.

2) Found
One smallish notebook, unruled paper, dog-eared leaves, much discolouring (some staining). Contents: pencil scribbles, ramblings and doodles to most pages including amateurish cartoon profiles and caricatures, juvenilia, doggerel and shopping lists in a childish hand, plus evidence of train-spotting. Distinct whiff of alehouse. Some bite-marks. Also contains occasional profanities, questionable theological statements and crude anatomical representations (Parish Magistrate duly notified). Recovered from wasteland near the Lord Nelson Inn, Luddenden Foot, along with masonic apparatus (see separate listing) and bloody handkerchief (incinerated upon discovery). Assumed local owner. No intrinsic worth but of some personal or sentimental value, possibly. To be held for one week only.

Little Henry

This is the story
   of poor Little Henry:
begotten on Thursday,
   beloved on Friday,
bereaved on Saturday,
   believed on Sunday,
beleaguered on Monday,
   besotted on Tuesday,
belittled on Wednesday,
   besmirched on Thursday,
befuddled on Friday,
   bedevilled on Saturday,
becalmed on Sunday.
   Poor Little Henry,
that was his story.

The Gos Hawk

after Thomas Bewick

This fplendid creature,
   though thoroughly native,
   is feldom feen
in our fields and forefts.

The male of the fpecies
   is fmaller but more vicious,
   feeding on mice
and birdlings, plucking and tearing

and fwallowing pieces whole
   then later difgorging
   pellets of hair,
fur, feathers and indigeftible bones.

In the Far Eaft, fuch predators
   are authority's fymbol
   when flown from the arm
of the Great Emperor's grand falconer,

and a fight to behold, doubtlefs,
   by thofe many thoufands
   of inferior rank
who are fervants and followers.

In olden times
   the cuftom and practife
   of fporting a hawk
was confined to thofe perfons

of true means and proud definition,
   for a man might be known
   by his hawk
and his horfe and alfo his hound,

though ladies too
   are fomtimes depicted
   with hawks at their wrifts,
bearing their raptors thufly.

Of high eftimation, neverthelefs
   the bird is renowned
   for its indolent traits
and lack of courage, compared

to the Merlin, Hobby or Jer-Falcon,
   its longer-tailed, fwifter
   and (fome would fay)
more coveted, illuftrious coufins.

51–53
Poems
Armitage
Features
Armitage
Butcher

The End

So death comes as a death-like figure.
You thought its shape in the long meadow
was a stone gatepost or dwarf elder,
but made the fatal mistake one evening
of catching its eye, staring too deeply.
At which moment it stepped forward.

True, you can outpace it, no problem,
stay miles ahead of its cheese-wire garland,
years in front of the chloroform nosebag.
Also true, you have in your favour
a tongue dripping with liquid silver,
the cute looks of a Celtic Jesus,

spring-heeled boots and that polished sovereign
hooked from your sleeping father's pocket.
But death keeps on stalking, drawn onwards,
not stopped or stalled by gritstone or gable,
till the night comes when your mind's too brittle
to grip and twist the childproof bottle:

downstairs you hear the back door open
and close, footfall in the flagged hallway,
a mock scream from that warped floorboard
outside the bedroom. You roll over
and face the wall, just lie there frozen
watching its scrawny shadow rise and harden.

Verdopolis

A deathbed dream:
I've strolled unchallenged
past merchants' houses
to an arched bridge

medieval in structure,
the glazed river sliding away
underneath, behind me
a duomo or domed palazzo:

it ain't Bradford.
The next scene's a tad sketchy
(a moat? portcullis?):
inside the island-chateau

I've climbed
the spiral timber stairs
of the highest tower
to a lantern-turret

to paint the landscape.
But in that instant
all the words I've ever written
rise and flap

like panicked birds,
choking the sky, and letters
wuther like black snow
in the final blizzard.

On 'Mansions in the Sky:
The Rise and Fall of Branwell Brontë'

Curated by Simon Armitage. The Brontë Parsonage Museum, 1 February 2017 – 1 January 2018

EMMA BUTCHER

Patrick Branwell Brontë: dreamer, writer, artist, addict, failure – brother of the three famous Brontë sisters. This year marks the bicentenary of his birth and Simon Armitage, together with the Brontë Parsonage Museum, has been reflecting on this young romantic's fantasies and dark, lonely demise. Armitage has produced ten new poems and presented them alongside Branwell's belongings in the Parsonage's new exhibition 'Mansions in the Sky'. Each gives us the opportunity to connect with this reprobate of history who strove for stardom, yet died unrecognised and unfulfilled. Through each reading, we experience Branwell as a modern figure, a person who reminds us of someone we know, someone in our family, or whom we ourselves once were. At points, Armitage is deliberately anachronistic – he references Paul Pogba, The Smiths, Facebook – at other points, he plays with language and tone to bring Branwell into our hearts; to recognise his flaws, but celebrate his wild and charismatic presence within the family unit. But in order to truly understand why he resonates, we need to understand his life. Throughout this brief biography, I mark moments where Armitage's poems have brought new, contemporary meaning to the 'black sheep' of the Brontë world.

BRANWELL BRONTË: A LIFE
(ARMITAGE: 'SELF PORTRAIT')

Branwell, was born in 1817 in the Yorkshire village of Haworth, the son of the learned curate, the Reverend Patrick Brontë and the brother of Charlotte, Emily and Anne Brontë, the famous Victorian authors. He grew up in the local parsonage, which backed on to the windswept, open moors. Growing up, the children were encouraged to embrace their creative impulses and inspirations, using the moors as a canvas to explore their growing love of adventure, the arts, and the natural world (Armitage: 'Gos Hawk'). From 1826, the young Brontë siblings nurtured each other's writing talents. Using toy characters, they created complex fantasy kingdoms, collaborating on an intricate network of characters, places and events (Armitage: 'Little Henry'). In varying forms, these kingdoms would become individually known as the Glass Town, Angria and Gondal (Armitage: 'Verdopolis'). A majority of the siblings' inspiration would come from what they read. Using all manners of literary material, ranging from contemporary periodicals to classical texts, they would rework histories and current affairs into their worlds, creating a self-absorbed saga based on their own playful, imaginative responses (Armitage: 'The Smallprint'). Branwell was central to these kingdoms, dictating the linear chronology of events; his enthusiasm and cheerful nature shines through his manuscripts. He was a well-informed, intelligent commentator of the world around him with an impressive grasp on language and varying genres, especially satirical sketches. This was only emphasised by his passion for masculine pursuits such as pugilism, club culture, and freemasonry (Armitage: 'Initiation'). Over time, Branwell's boldness and arrogance grew: he was chief of his literary sibling unit and he was well aware of his small microcosm of power.

His overconfidence, however, would be his downfall. He aspired to be a great poet, yet his boastful, somewhat erratic nature prevented him exercising the control and patience necessary to achieve such lofty heights. His passion for writing would often develop into an imitative, exuberant and obsessive mania and he struggled to find his own unique voice. Over the years, Branwell tried to communicate with a number of successful writers, sending them copies of his poems and transcriptions. In 1836, the hopeful nineteen-year-old sent one of his poems to William Wordsworth along with a letter expressing his hopes and dreams of building mansions in the sky, to 'push out into the open world'. Wordsworth did not reply (Armitage: 'William, It Was Really Nothing'). In the 1840s, a similar silence was followed by Thomas De Quincey and the editors of *Blackwood's Edinburgh Magazine*. He did, however, receive encouragement from Hartley Coleridge, but even their correspondence eventually ground to a halt. Nevertheless, despite repeated rejections, which were often bitterly internalised, he was the first published out of his literary siblings. His poems, written under his Angrian pseudonym, Northangerland, were published in local and national newspapers. This was, however, as far as his ambitions would take him.

With his writing career stagnant and pressure mounting to provide for his family, Branwell took on various occupations that ranged from tutoring to being a railway clerk (Armitage: 'Lost and Found'). At every turn, however, he would rebel against his responsibilities by going on excessive drinking sprees down the local pub, or conducting affairs with married women. There were even rumours that, in 1845, he was dismissed from his last place of employment, Thorp Green, after indulging in an illicit relationship with the lady of the house, Lydia Robinson, who was nearly fifteen years his senior. In a letter to his friends, Branwell, in his usual cocky manner, wrote 'my mistress is DAMNBLY TOO FOND OF ME'. Indeed, he soon found out she was not. After his dismissal and his final journey back to the family home, she refused to continue relations with Branwell, sending him into a spiral of debt and depression with an intractable addition to drugs and alcohol. This would ultimately led to his death (Armitage: 'Wallet'). In the last years of his life he was a source of anguish and embarrassment for his family. His father felt his demise keenly, especially when his son's volatile behaviour forced him to keep watch over him every night to ensure he did not set his bed on fire. In his final months, Branwell was sending scraps of paper to friends asking for 'five pence worth of Gin'. He drew a sketch of himself writhing around on his deathbed; a skeleton looms over him, its hand outstretched to snatch him away from the world (Armitage: 'The End'). In 1848, Branwell died from the long-term effects of substance abuse. It is rumoured that he retained his inflated ego right until death took hold, insisting that he should die standing up to demonstrate the power of human will. He died crying out 'In all my passed life I have done nothing either great or good'. After the ordeal, his sister Charlotte did not weep for him, but 'for the wreck of talent' and 'the ruin of promise'. These words are all the more acute as we remember him as a footnote of his sisters' celebrated legacy. Simon's poems allow us to come to terms with and embrace Branwell's lesser place alongside them, but equally, they etch a new, important place for Branwell in history that affirms his human qualities and appreciates his frenzied determination.

Beginning with Endings

An Essay on Prosody

CHRIS MCCULLY

WHAT FOLLOWS IS AN ESSAY about versification – prosody, to give the subject its older title. The first two sections of the essay touch on linguistic metrics; these sections are precursors to the three final sections of the piece, all of which treat in different ways of the notion of metrical *constraints*, particularly as those have been expressed in a version of linguistic metrics current since the later 1990s, namely Optimality Theory (OT). I've written about this here because OT-based forms of thinking about metrical (and non-metrical) organisation seem intuitively quite satisfying to me *as a writer of verse*. It is primarily as a writer, secondarily as a writer-and-reader, and not at all as a linguistic specialist or critic, that I have put these thoughts into their present form.

So as not to clutter up the piece with foot- or endnotes I summarise here some of those works from which the piece derives. The source for OT is often and with justice cited as Alan Prince and Paul Smolensky, *Optimality Theory: Constraint Interaction in Generative Grammar*, Technical Report number 2, Rutgers Centre for Cognitive Science (1993), also available in the Rutgers Optimality Archive, ROA 537-0802. In the same period Alan Prince was also doing important work with John McCarthy, e.g. the paper 'Generalized alignment' in Geert Booij and Jaap van Marle (eds.), *Yearbook of Morphology 1993* (Dordrecht: Kluwer, pp. 79–153). OT reached the textbooks in Diana Archangeli and Terence Langendoen (eds.) *Optimality Theory: An Overview* (Oxford: Blackwell, 1997) and in a fuller form in René Kager's *Optimality Theory* (Cambridge: Cambridge University Press, 1999). Chapter 11, and especially section 11.5ff., of Chris McCully, *The Sound Structure of English* (Cambridge: Cambridge University Press, 2009) offers a brief and basic introduction to OT.

Much earlier linguistic metrics looked back in some form or other to Noam Chomsky and Morris Halle, *The Sound Pattern of English* (New York: Harper and Row, 1968). Earlier (and later) versions both of classic linguistics and structuralism of course referenced Saussure (though Chomsky's notion of what was then called 'deep structure' shouldn't be taken to be isomorphic with Saussure's 'langue'). The best recent translation I know of Saussure's 1916 *Cours de Linguistique Générale* is that of Roy Harris (*Course in General Linguistics*, London: Duckworth, 1983); see also Jonathan Culler, *Saussure* (London: Fontana/Collins, 1976, p. 27.) Saussure's view of the indivisibility of signifier and signified has been too little noticed: 'Each sign is a dual entity, uniting signal [*signifiant* – McC] with signification (*signifié*). Neither facet of this duality exists independently of the other...' (Roy Harris, translator's introduction, *Course in General Linguistics*, London: Duckworth, 1983, p. xi). In 'Nature of the linguistic sign' (pp. 65–70 of Harris's edition) Saussure also insisted that although the sign itself may be arbitrary it nevertheless comprised a 'two-sided psychological entity' whose two elements, concept and sound pattern, 'are intimately linked and each triggers the other' (p. 66 of Roy Harris's translation of the *Cours*). There is no 'free play of the signifier' here.

Morris Halle and Nigel Fabb's *Meter in Poetry* appeared in 2008 (Cambridge: Cambridge University Press). In the thirty years preceding the appearance of *Meter in Poetry* a number of important papers and books had appeared in the field. These include e.g. Paul Kiparsky and G. Youmans (eds.) *Phonetics and Phonology. Vol. 1: Rhythm and Meter* (San Diego: Academic Press, 1989) and C. B. McCully and J. J. Anderson (eds.) *English Historical Metrics* (Cambridge: Cambridge University Press, 1996). There's also an important universalist modulation of metrics in Kristin Hanson and Paul Kiparsky, 1996: 'A parametric theory of poetic meter,' *Language* 72/2, pp. 287–353. More recently, a section of Denison et al. (eds.) *Analysing Older English* (Cambridge: Cambridge University Press, 2012), is devoted to 'Metrics and onomastics in older English' (Part 1, pp. 7–55).

Work in the field of what is inaccurately called 'metrical phonology' looks back to Mark Liberman and Alan Prince 1977, 'On stress and linguistic rhythm,' *Linguistic Inquiry* 8, pp. 249–33. Bruce Hayes, *Metrical Stress Theory: Principles and Case Studies* (London: University of Chicago Press, 1995) is a brilliant exposition of linguistic stress theory. The principles governing the stressing of words is also explored in Harry van der Hulst (ed.) *Word Prosodic Systems in the Languages of Europe* (Berlin: Mouton de Gruyter, 1999). An overview of 'metrical phonology' together with tree- and grid-based representations of rhythm and word-stress, is given in Chris McCully, 'Metrical phonology' in *Encyclopedia of Language and Linguistics* (Amsterdam: Elsevier, 2006, pp. 113–119). Staying with the generativist linguistic context, Fred Lerdahl and Ray Jackendoff explored *A Generative Theory of Tonal Music* (Cambridge, MA: MIT Press, 1983) and Paul Kiparsky published an influential paper on metrics in 1977 ('The linguistic structure of English verse', *Linguistic Inquiry* 8/2: 189–247).

I have side-stepped a number of important questions in this initial sketch of OT-based metrics, in particular the question as to whether a poet *intends to produce* a well-formed 'output' and, accordingly, whether metrical constraints are in principle different from other linguistic constraints. That is, the goal of standard OT grammars is derivation; it's not clear that the goal of metrics should be derivation or whether OT-based metrics should simply attempt to characterise a set of judgements about the metricality or otherwise of lines of verse. This matter is wonderfully well explored in Bruce Hayes, 'Faithfulness and componentiality in metrics', a piece that first appeared in the Rutgers Optimality Archive (2000) but which was electronically published for general readers two years later (www.linguistics.ucla.edu/people/hayes/ FaithfulnessInMetrics/FaithfulnessInMetrics.PDF).

A possible constraint ranking for classical Old English alliterative verse is explored in chapter 5 of Chris McCully and Sharon Hilles, *The Earliest English* (London: Pearson, 2005).

The most recent (and linguistically sophisticated) history of English prosody known to me is Martin J. Duffell, *A New History of English Metre* (Oxford: Legenda, Studies in Linguistics 5, Modern Humanities Research Association and Maney Publishing, 2008).

*

METRICS, RULES & UNDERLYING STRUCTURE

Many years ago I was invited to share a podium with two professors who were then working at the University of Manchester. Our remit was to sketch recent research developments in the field of English studies to an audience of graduates and others. I did not then often receive, and have since rarely received, invitations to appear on seminar platforms with the great and good. I suppose I was there to make up numbers. Nevertheless, I prepared what I had to say together with a paper handout sufficient for forty attendees. I imagined it might be interesting – even in such distinguished company, even to an audience which held literary and cultural-theoretical specialists of different persuasions – if I were to attempt to outline recent developments in theoretical linguistics and notably, the impact that Optimality Theory (OT) was then having on views of the standard linguistic model of how sound-structure – indeed, how language in general – was organised.

The podium filled; the room pumped up with breath. The professors conversed. Memory tells that there was some earnest interrogation of that dear old suspect, How Meaning Could Mean. How Meaning Could Mean was apparently much to our audience's taste – and (one might say) why not?

When my turn came to speak I had sand in my throat. I explained, by way of introduction, that a disconcerting question had followed me about all my life: *Why am I here?* I felt under-equipped to revisit Ogden and Richards (*The Meaning of Meaning*, London, 1923 and many times subsequently reprinted). I felt under-equipped to revisit almost anything – except to try dumbly to fulfil the terms that had brought me to the podium. I went on, in the allotted time, to attempt a too-brief explanation of the workings of OT and their consequences to an ever-more mystified audience. Although it was too early, I said, to state that the coming of OT was an instance of paradigm shift, the impact that OT was having, not least in the fields of sound-structure and prosody, compelled a re-examination of ideas such as underlying structure and indeed the concept of derivation itself.

What interested me then and what interests me still is that OT provides a new way of conceiving the relationship between the underlying structure of a language and how that structure appears in speech. In the standard linguistic model of phonology, which reached then-classic exposition in Noam Chomsky and Morris Halle's *The Sound Pattern of English* (New York, 1968), underlying forms (phonemes) are, in their passage to utterance, derived by an ordered set of rules so that they become well-formed surface sounds, the (allo)phones of speech. What a phonological rule does, in effect, is take an underlying piece of structure and tell it what to become. A trivial example: there is an underlying speech-sound /p/ in English. In words such as *pin, pat, pet*, however (unlike in words such as *nip, stop* or *clasp*), the underlying /p/ appears in speech with strong aspiration. Why? In the standard model there is a rule which instructs the phoneme to behave in a certain way in a certain environment: 'When occurring initially in a stressed syllable, you will acquire aspiration'. Such a rule, which should in principle apply exceptionlessly, predicts that in the appropriate environment, i.e. initially in a stressed syllable, /p/ appears as surface [pʰ].

Thus conceived, the underlying structure of a language bears some resemblance to what Saussure explained as *langue*, the *system* of that language. The actually-occurring forms of language (in speech or writing) Saussure called *parole*. Saussure made use of homely analogies to emphasise his view of *langue*, of which my favourite is that of the train. *Langue* is equivalent to the timetable of trains, not the trains themselves. The elements that comprise *langue* are therefore abstract, just as a train timetable is, formally speaking, abstract. Nor does the train timetable know or care whether the trains are painted red or yellow or have two carriages or sixteen. Yet Saussure also made the crucial point that *langue* and *parole* aren't separable: they're as indivisible as two sides of a single sheet of paper.

The underlying and the actually-occurring, the relationship between the two, how presence could be derived from abstraction, how linguistic rules worked or failed to work: I became interested in such matters thirty-five years ago and a related interest sustained some of my research in the 1980s and 90s. In those decades, it seemed a common experience in the United Kingdom for university departments of English, which had once been broad churches containing close readers, critical theoreticians, philologists and theoretical linguists, to polarise, even to split formally, into separate departments comprising, on the one hand, specialists in literatures and different kinds of cultural and critical theory, and on the other, remaining philologists and linguistic theoreticians and historians. For a while, (post-) structuralism – which could in a crude sense be viewed as an unlovely variant of *close-reading-with-semiology* – provided a perhaps unlikely bridge between language specialists and literary critics but I think it is generally true to say that the bridge, which had never been particularly steady in the first place, eventually gave way. The result has been that the recent and current work of many linguists and language historians, including those working professionally on the English language, has seemed to become ever more invisible to those working on or with English literature or in those fields of cultural theory related to English literature. This parting of the ways, if it was a parting of the ways, is in my view a pity. There's much still to discuss, much yet to do.

RULE-BASED PROSODY:
HALLE & FABB (2008)

Over the past forty years some important work has been done by linguists on many aspects of poetic form, to the extent that work on English prosody in particular – a field now often dubbed 'metrics' to disambiguate it from analyses of other aspects of sound-structure such as the internal organisation of syllables – has attracted research monographs or collections of papers emanating from symposia. In the same period, linguistic research into the nature and description of rhythmicity in the world's languages has been extensive and a number of competing linguistic models for the representation of rhythmicity – tree-based, grid-based or hybrid models – have been deployed or discarded. Such enterprise, which as far as the representation of verse prosodies is concerned was never particularly unified, reached further expression in Nigel Fabb and Morris Halle's *Meter in Poetry*, which adopts a grid-based, parameterised model through which to describe the major metres of seven of the world's languages or language-families. The ambition of this important work is clearly universalist (other of the world's metres can in principle be described by applying a grid-based and parameterised model) and is also refreshingly aware of the interdisciplinary potential of its methodology: Appendix A of chapter 1, for instance, explicitly relates the description of poetic metres to music ('[M]usical meters are constructed by iterative rules of parenthesis insertion of the same kind as those employed above in assigning metrical grids to lines of poetry,' p. 36 – Fabb and Halle's primary example, the opening of Mozart's *Symphony No. 40*, is derived from Lerdahl and Jackendoff, 1983). Noteworthy, too, is the authors' awareness of poetic forms whose structure is, strictly-speaking, non-metrical but whose existence depends of various kinds of rhythmical or syntactic parallelism.

Fabb and Halle's central principle is that for a metre to exist at all, something must be *counted*. Something must, therefore, be *measured*. In metrical verse, what is counted and measured are not only poetic *lines*, where 'line' is a constituent unique to poetry, but also *groupings* that comprise the lines. Where the number of adjacent lines are measured one may, if those lines are constructed as equivalent in terms of their internal groupings, discern a stanza, particularly since rhyme schemes, when they are used in patterned ways, themselves imply measurement. So, trivially, the octave of e.g. a Shakespearean sonnet would comprise eight lines, the sestet six. Less trivially, because lines of stanzas are built out of equivalent structures, the stanza is in principle parellelistic: the aesthetic effect of the stanza is one of expected or deferred cumulation.

Groupings are conceived in Fabb and Halle's view (p. 4) as projections of syllables – projections into a metrical grid that is then subject to iterative and projective principles that appear to build rhythmical and metrical structure into the line being analysed but which are better conceived as describing rhythmical and metrical structure already present in the line. This may be illustrated through borrowing a partial description of one of Fabb and Halle's introductory examples, the line 'Ever let the Fancy roam' (Keats).

1. Project each syllable into a gridline:
   Ever let the Fancy roam
   *   *   *   *   *   *   *

2. Group the projections (via the application of a rule which iterates across the projections):
   Ever let the Fancy roam
   (* * (*   *   (*   *   (*

3. Project the head of each group onto a new gridline (via the application of a rule which specifies which projection is selected to be the head of each group)
   Ever let the Fancy roam
   (* * (*   *   (*   *   (*
    *   *   *   *

Further gridlines are then constructed, again depending on the application of parameterised rules; the final gridline must span exactly one asterisk – something stipulated in a condition on the construction of well-formed metrical grids. In this procedure, the analysis of a metrical line 'is determined on the one hand by the size of groups on each gridline, and on the other hand by the number of gridlines for which rules of syllable grouping are specified' (Fabb and Halle, p. 7). Further, grids are essentially abstract: computed line-by-line, they are patterns which 'determine [...] the perception of syllables as a line of metrical verse' (p. 11). Further, the computations which organise grids consist of 'the ordered application of a licensed set of rules' (p. 11, where a set of rules 'is "licensed" when it is observed by a poetic school or tradition').

I find many things to admire in Fabb and Halle's text, not least their description of both Manley Hopkins' regular iambic verse (pp. 82–85) and his verse evincing sprung rhythm (an innovation which allows for the non-projection of syllables into grids, pp. 85–90). The basal emphasis on counting and measurement is clearly correct – it is the same impulse which joins poetry with music and with dance – and the universalist ambition admirable. Yet I also found myself questioning whether this model was intuitively satisfying to me *as a writer* of verse. Years before, I had privately asked myself the same question when exploring Paul Kiparsky's influential 1977 paper on the organisation of English metre, in which he suggested (a) that there were both bracketing and labelling mismatches to be found between the underlying structure of a line of verse and the linguistic material actually filling that same line, and (b) that the (metrical) complexity of a line could be calculated from the number of mismatches in it (1977, p. 195). While it was ingenious to have access to such a matrix of complexity, was I conscious *as a writer* (I asked myself) of those principles? Were such principles intuitively satisfying?

At the same time as querying my intuitions as a writer I also wondered about the 'ordered application' of a 'licensed set of rules' that is so vital to Fabb and Halle's 2008 analysis of metres. At almost the same time as I was encountering Fabb and Halle's text I was also writing specifically about the problem of rule-application in a short textbook on English phonology. Suppose, for example, one wished to derive a surface form [XCZ] from an underlying form /XAY/. Three ordered rules would have to apply: A would have to become B in a specified context; then Y would have to become Z in a specified context; finally, B would have to become C in a specified context. Following Kager (1999, p. 58), I gave the following figure and brief description:

Underlying form: /XAY/

Rule 1: A → B/X_____
    Intermediate form   XBY
Rule 2: Y → Z/B_____
    Intermediate form   XBZ
Rule 3: B → C/X_____Z
    Intermediate form   XCZ

Surface form: [XCZ]

Note that the rules have to apply in the order given so that the correct surface form is derived. (How do the rules know how to order themselves? Can rules 'conspire'?) Our problem, however, is crucially that the intermediate form XBZ isn't immediately inferable from *either* the underlying *or* the surface form. That intermediate form is simply mechanically generated as an inevitable part of a process, and – since it has no easily inferable relationship to either underlying or surface forms – is said to be *opaque*.

A key question to ask at this point is this: *how can any speaker ever learn such opaque forms?* If they are 'true', these intermediate forms are certainly parts of the linguistic competence of a given speaker, but since it relies on *opacity*, then *how can such a system ever be learned?*

This worry about opacity met my prior worry about how intuitively satisfying rule-based metrical analyses were. What did I actually *do*, when I was composing and revising verse? How had I learned those metrical or non-metrical principles that manifested themselves in the poetry I had written? Was I aware of metrical complexity in the course of composition? Did I proceed, in composition, grouping by grouping – or was the emergence of so many pencil scribblings, false starts and erasures in my poetry workbooks a symptom of the baleful working-out of different processes?

COUNTING, CLOSURE AND CONSTRAINTS
When I'm writing verse it's rare for me to proceed syllable-by-syllable or (it may be) foot-by-foot. Sometimes, as in metrical translations of Old English verse (Chris McCully, *Old English Poems and Riddles*. Manchester: Carcanet, 2008), it's been necessary to consider the form of particular light or heavy syllable against the requirements of an underlying metrical template but I rarely consider these matters when composing contemporary verse. What concern me when I'm writing metrical verse seem to be (i) an overall sense of syllable count and the line, (ii) line-breaks and (iii) thematic and metrical freedom. (Appropriacy of diction is another great concern, of course, but the poetry workbooks suggest that words are rejected or replaced towards the end of the process of metrical composition. By this I don't

intend to imply that diction is unimportant. In fact, the underlying (metrical) structure of some poems-to-be may be triggered by the phonotactics of words themselves, even if the triggering words are subsquently changed or deleted at a later stage of the drafting process.)

The previous paragraph should not be taken to mean that in composing verse I sit down and imagine that 'Today, I'm going to compose something in the form of a Shakespearean sonnet'. Far from it. Something else seems to take place in the moments of composition. I've already said that 'the line', line-breaks and thematic and metrical freedom seem essential to my own ways of working, but can I be any more specific and critically satisfying than that?

What, more precisely, is a poet's 'sense of "the line"'? (I emphasise again that I'm here speaking only of metrical verse, though these remarks also bear, I think, on *vers libéré* – 'freed verse' whose freedom consists chiefly in playing against a stricter underlying metrical form.) A line is among other things a metrical domain. And what is a metrical domain? *A metrical domain is an underlyingly closed structure between whose constituent parts various constraints operate.*

It's appropriate to say something about *constraints* as these are conceived in OT and as they may have bearing on the process of verse composition. In the standard model of OT, the production of well-formed language involves *evaluation of forms*. Language is organised such that an input is generated ('GEN' below) together with a competing list of rival forms into an evaluative process ('EVAL' below) which consists of a set of constraints. The constraints select the winning candidate from among the competing input forms, so that a well-formed output is selected. There's great freedom in this process – the candidate set assessed under GEN can be comprised by any sort of linguistic object – yet encoded into the scheme there's also the principled notion that outputs should correspond as closely as possible to inputs.

Evaluation of forms in OT

		GEN	EVAL	
Underlying		ABC		Surface (Output)
(Input)		ABD	Constraints	
		AB		
/ABC/	→ → →	BCF	→ → →	[ABC]
		XZE		
		XPCE		
		XZWE		
		Brrrr!		
		Sssssss!		
		....		

Unlike linguistic rules, which apply automatically wherever their structural descriptions are met, constraints are in principle *violable*. As I put the matter in *The Sound Structure of English* (p. 201), 'constraints are *ranked*, such that candidates are *the better formed, the fewer higher-ranked constraints they violate*'.

In a verse-prosodic context, suppose that there are two constraints that apply to the evaluation of the (English) iambic pentameter. One constraint concerns how these lines end. It is therefore a *closure* constraint: the tenth syllable of the line must be filled by a stressed syllable. The second constraint is a *counting* constraint: each (English) pentametric line must contain exactly ten syllables. The much-cited Shakespearean line 'Of hand, of foot, of lip, of eye, of brow' (*Sonnet* 106) violates neither of these constraints and is for these reasons (as well as several others) perfectly formed. Yet as everyone knows, not all pentametric lines consist of exactly ten syllables. Some frequent variants span eleven syllables:

But day doth daily draw my sorrows longer,
And night doth nightly make grief's length seem stronger.
(*Sonnet* 28)

Yet him for this my love no whit disdaineth;
Suns of the world may stain when heaven's sun staineth.
(*Sonnet* 33)

And other common variants of the pentameter span nine syllables (so-called 'headless lines'):

Stay, the King hath thrown his warder down
(*Richard II*, Act 1, scene 3)

An important notion here is that of the relative importance of the constraints evaluating the metrical line: it seems more important that lines should conform to the requirement that their tenth syllable is stressed than that they should contain exactly ten syllables. Note also that a headless line would, if it contained an initial (unstressed) syllable, be a perfectly well-formed pentametric line. That implies two further things about the construction of metrical lines: (a) metrical constituents within a line must be filled and (b) there is more freedom (e.g. to omit syllables and/or violate other constraints) in the opening of a metrical line than at the end.

Count, close, fill & free

We now seem to be dealing with four possible constraints that bear on evaluating well-formed pentametric lines. The first is a constraint on counting (COUNT). The second is a constraint on closure (CLOSE). The third is a constraint on filling (FILL) and the last a constraint on metrical freedom which the linguist Bruce Hayes has characterised as 'beginnings free, endings strict' (a constraint I shall here call, in shorthand, FREE). In the few examples noted above it would seem to be the case that:

CLOSE is never violated and is therefore more important than COUNT
FILL (and COUNT) may be violated if FREE is not.

That suggests a possible ranking of these metrical constraints. If we allow the symbol '>' to stand for 'is more important than' then the following ranking is conceivable:

CLOSE > COUNT > FREE > FILL

Suppose we had a different ranking, FILL > COUNT > FREE > CLOSE. That would mean that it would

be impossible ever to have headless lines (since all metrical positions, including the first within the line, would have to be filled) and also, because COUNT > FREE > CLOSE, that hendacasyllabic variants would never occur within any pentameter. In other words, such a possible ranking would be both counter-factual and counter-intuitive.

The two possible metrical constraints CLOSE and COUNT allow for the characterisation of a surprisingly extensive range of different kinds of verse structure, and not just metrical verse structure. Under an OT-style schema it would be possible to have verse that exhibited COUNT > CLOSE. This would mean 'it's more important for metrical domains to span exactly a given number of syllables /other constituents than it is for those domains to end in particular ways'. An example here would be syllabic verse in English – haiku is one instance. It seems important to note, however, that haiku doesn't provide an instance of 'free verse'. How could it? Something is counted, even if that something isn't, in metrical terms, closed. Therefore haiku affords an example of 'freed verse' – *verse libéré*, not *vers libre*.

A further example of *verse libéré* would be the following, from William Carlos Williams. Suppose, for instance, that what a closure constraint required was for the rightmost edges of verse lines to be adjacent to syntactic boundaries. Now consider the following:

so much depends
upon
a red wheel
barrow
glazed with rain
water
beside the white
chickens

The verb *depends* is immediately followed by a syntactic boundary, i.e. the boundary that delimits the left edge of the prepositional phrase 'upon... chickens'. The preposition *upon* is followed by a syntactic boundary, i.e. the one that introduces the noun phrase 'a red wheel barrow'. In the following lines, the noun phrases '(a red) wheel barrow', '(with) rain water' and '(beside the) white chickens' each contain a head noun (*barrow*, *water*, *chickens*) which is pre-modified by either another noun ('wheel', 'rain') or an adjective ('white'). The syntactic structure of such compound nouns or syntactic phrases is roughly as follows:

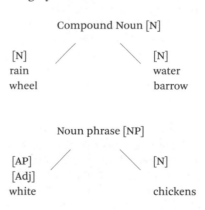

Compound Noun [N]

[N]   [N]
rain   water
wheel   barrow

Noun phrase [NP]

[AP]   [N]
[Adj]
white   chickens

In both cases, however, there is a boundary – lexical and/or phrasal – between the modifier and the head noun. And last, the final word of the poem, 'chickens', is followed by a closing syntactic boundary.

There's also a counting constraint at work in the poem:

so much depends	syllable count:	4
upon		2
a red wheel		3
barrow		2
glazed with rain		3
water		2
beside the white		4
chickens		2

The constraint: 'Every other (i.e. even-numbered) line of the poem must span exactly two syllables'. This isn't I think a *metrical* constraint: it doesn't apply across every line. It's simply a counting constraint that applies to this particular poem. Yet it's a constraint nevertheless and as such leads to the suspicion that the form Williams deploys employs both CLOSE and (partially, perhaps idiosyncratically) COUNT. (The reader might also note that the two main clauses of the poem each span eleven syllables; haunting those eleven-syllable spans is perhaps the ghost of the pentameter.)

These remarks lead to the suspicion that the separation of 'metrical' from 'nonmetrical' verse isn't clear-cut. In fact, if the foregoing is along the right lines then a cline of metricality could be envisioned:

Least metrical	More metrical	More metrical	Fully metrical
Most prose-like	Less prose-like	Less prose-like	Least prose-like

No COUNT	COUNT	CLOSE	COUNT
No CLOSE	No CLOSE	No COUNT	CLOSE

Some manifestations of these possible categories of verse: (a) non-COUNT, non-CLOSE verse would be 'free verse' – *vers libre*. Structurally, some kinds of such verse would be, when spoken, impossible to distinguish from prose. (b) Verse that is counted but not closed is exemplified in the haiku, tanka and other syllabic forms. (c) Verse that is closed but not counted is exemplified in the pantoum, where the lines (metrical domains) may in principle by of any length (thus non-COUNT) but where the lines fall into strict groupings (quatrains) and are subject to strict repetition (a manifestation of CLOSE). (d) Verse that is fully metrical is both counted and closed. To familiar examples such as iambic pentameter, tetrameter and so forth I'd also add Old English alliterative verse, which is in my view constructed around two high-ranked constraints, one that states that each half-line consists of four metrical positions (COUNT), the other requiring that half-lines end in certain ways (CLOSE).

*

CONSTRAINTS AND CREATIVE INTUITION

I'm conscious that the foregoing will seem almost childishly simple to any theoretical linguists reading even this far. Yet the central point I'm trying to explore seems to me worth repeating: it may well be the case that prosody is more dynamic than many writers and critics have hitherto imagined and is dynamic precisely because the generation and apprehension of metrical (and some less metrical) lines may well turn out to depend on the creative interaction of metrical constraints. Even in the foregoing we've begun to imagine how powerful this set of characterisations of prosody can be and it has even helped us towards understanding not an absolute distinction between 'metrical' and 'free' verse but a far more interesting cline that spans the fully metrical to the most prose-like.

There's one particularly interesting thing about this that engages me as a writer. For all kinds of metrical verse, CLOSE seems to be the highest-ranked constraint and metrical freedom is greatest at the openings of metrical constituents. Yet CLOSE can't exist in isolation. Take the pentameter again. If the tenth syllable of the pentametric line is filled by some kind of stressed syllable then the ninth syllable of the same line must be filled by a syllable bearing less stress than the tenth. Furthermore, since metrical strictness (instantiated in the relative freedom to invert feet or play other structural tricks) is greatest towards the line end then it would seem very likely that the eighth syllable of the metrical pentameter would bear more stress than the ninth. And if *that* were the case then the seventh syllable of the line would almost invariably display less stress than the eighth syllable. In short, the interaction between CLOSE and FREE ('beginnings free, endings strict') determines that pentametric lines will tend almost always to end 'de-DUM de-DUM' – that is, metrical closure involves a *dynamic*. What happens metrically and syntactically as lines end and turn has an effect earlier in the line, and this makes sense to me as a writer: I may not be – I very rarely am – conscious of metred language as a matching of linguistic material against an abstract set of positions but I'm certainly conscious of lines and their succession as a sequence of acoustic and semantic dynamics.

*

CLOSING WITH CLOSURE

If I speak purely as a writer of verse then over the years there have been a mere handful of critical works I've found useful. One is Barbara Herrnstein Smith's *Poetic Closure* (Chicago University Press, 1968). Smith makes the point that humans are pattern-making and pattern-perceiving creatures: a truism, but one that becomes more interesting if one believes that readers engage in 'retrospective patterning' (p.13) when our expectations of sequences are disrupted. Take the following:

ABABCDCDEFEF (etc.) – what is the pattern? What are our expectations?

ABACADAEAF (etc.) – what is the pattern? What are our expectations?

The first C in each sequence is disruptive. We engage in retrospective patterning precisely when a sequence is disrupted.

Further, as Smith points out, closure doesn't simply mean 'end'. For example, the structures of verbal art can be so carefully deployed (and the reader so manipulated) as to produce *the desire for closure*. This can be seen in much metrical poetry, where the closural device is a return to metrical regularity after metrical variation or disruption. Smith (p. 44) cites Herrick's 'To Electra':

I dare not ask a kisse;
I dare not beg a smile;
Lest having that, or this,
I might grow proud the while.

No, no, the utmost share
Of my desire, shall be
Onely to kisse that Aire,
That lately kissed Thee.

Note the relationship between line 7 (metrically disruptive, an effect that leads both to retrospection and to anticipation) and line 8 (the closural line, a return to the normative metrical pattern).

Closure, in Smith's view, may also be a matter of syntactic and phonological alignment, as in passages on Milton's blank verse, or even a semantic matter where a riddle or postulate is solved, as in certain epigrams or the punch-lines of some jokes. Above all, however, '[t]he perception of poetic structure is a dynamic process' (Smith, p. 33) – to which I only add that it is so, perhaps, because the *writing* of poetic structure is itself a dynamic process.

Thinking about prosodic closure isn't only a way of conceiving the structures of individual lines. The history of metrical inventiveness, the evolution (and death) of whole poetic genres, may also be described by reference to closure. One of the most important constraints on the highly-wrought, aristocratic verse of the Anglo-Saxons, for example, is precisely a constraint on metrical closure – on what sort of syllable can occur in the fourth position of the half-line. Barbara Strang put this most succinctly in her great *History of English* (London: Methuen, 1970), p. 326: '[T]here is between half-lines a break, or line-end marker [...] The end of a half-line is always determinate [...] [I]f it is occupied by a lift [stressed syllable – McC] that goes without saying, but if it is occupied by a drop there is the special restriction that the drop must there be monosyllabic'.

This closural constraint holds for almost all half-lines in the Anglo-Saxon corpus just as it holds for almost all Eddaic (and Old High German, Old Frisian) verse. Yet the effect of this special restriction (closural marker) is dynamic: if an unstressed syllable appears in the fourth position of a half-line then the immediately-preceding syllable must be some sort of stress, whether primary or secondary:

    sē þǣm heaðo-rincum
(who with those battle-men; -cum preceded by secondary stress; *Beowulf*, line 370a)
    fōn wið fēonde
(struggle against the demon; -de preceded by primary stress; *Beowulf*, line 439a)

Or again, to take a final example, and as Martin Duffell shows (p. 87ff. of his 2008 *History of English*

Metre), closure is a key to recognising the achievement of Chaucer in constructing the pentameter from his models, chiefly the *endacasillabo* of Boccaccio and Petrarch. For both Boccaccio and Petrarch it was possible to allow triple-rhythms both before a mid-line caesura and before the tenth syllable of the line. Thus Italian ten-syllable lines could both begin and end '(de-)de-de-DUM' (io de Parnaso le Muse pregare, *Filostrato* Book 1, example from Duffell, p.86, runs of unstressed material underlined): 'Chaucer's great innovation [...] was to elevate the iambic rhythm he found in an overwhelming majority of *endecasillabi* to a structural principal, and he did this by not placing lexically strong syllables in odd-numbered positions, and by placing stresses in most even-numbered ones' (Duffell, p. 87). By (almost wholly) ruling out triple-time closures, therefore, Chaucer single-handedly constructed 'the first true pentameters in any European language' (Duffell, p. 87). In these dynamics a new metre was born.

Many years have passed since I stood sand-tongued on that Manchester podium. What I wanted to say then consisted essentially of reaffirmation: underlying structure exists; OT can probably provide us with interesting ways of conceiving both the creation and perception of measured language; what we've so often called prosody is better conceived as a study of dynamics than the construction of rules. These years on, however, and for all the progress that has been made in the description of English and other verse prosodies, much remains to be accomplished. To the affirmations I wished to make a decade ago and for the work I think still remains to be done, I'd like to add a paradox: for poets as for prosodists, closure is no bad place to start.

'What is it like to be a cow?'

Kenneth Patchen, *The Journal of Albion Moonlight* (New Directions), $17.95

Reviewed by IAN SEED

It is good to see New Directions bringing out a new edition of *The Journal of Albion Moonlight*. Ironic too, given that the founding editor of New Directions, James Laughlin, initially rejected the book, describing it as a 'hopeless mess' and writing to Patchen in January 1941 that 'it would have damaged your reputation terribly' (see *Selected Correspondence of Kenneth Patchen*, Bottom Dog Press, 2012, p. 103). With the encouragement of Henry Miller, Robert Duncan and others, and the financial support of figures such as Wallace Stevens, Patchen had the book privately printed in June 1941, and eventually New Directions brought it out in 1946.

The *Journal of Albion Moonlight* takes as its inspiration the anonymous pre-Shakespearean poem, 'Tom o'Bedlam':

With an host of furious fancies
Whereof I am commander,
With a burning spear and a horse of air,
To the wilderness I wander.
By a knight of ghosts and shadows,
I summoned am to a tourney
Ten leagues beyond the wide world's end:
Methinks it is no journey.

From the beginning, we are taken into a crazy nightmarish otherworld. However, this otherworld is always intertwined with the political reality of the times: war was raging across Europe and all the talk was of whether the USA should come to Europe's rescue. Patchen took a deeply pacifist stance and indeed saw his book as a wakeup call to the world to stop its descent into self-destruction. The 'mess' of the book is intended to reflect the psychotic chaos that Patchen saw all around him. As Patchen himself wrote in a letter to Laughlin in August 1940, 'I had to recreate that chaos – whether I have done so will define my success or failure' (*Selected Correspondence of Kenneth Patchen*, p. 97). *The Journal of Albion Moonlight* charts an allegorical journey, switching continually between dream, memory, journalistic reportage, political polemic, religious exploration, literary parody, and poetic lyricism.

The appearance of the text on the page moves from straight prose to lineated poetry, sometimes presenting more than one column, or using different-sized fonts, and also playing with the white space on the page. We often forget now that Patchen was not only a pacifist poet, but also a continual experimenter with his fusing together of different art forms: for example, in his collaboration with a young John Cage in 1941, in his pioneering of poetry and jazz in the 1950s, and in his creation of visual poems. He is usually linked to the Beat poets, but can also be seen as a bridge between French surrealism and the New York poets, for example in the way he makes use of abrupt shifting registers of tone. Similarly, *The Journal of Albion Moonlight* has clear links to such fabulists as Russell Edson and the later James Tate. There are numerous dreamlike passages, stories within stories, which have an absurdist quality combined with a lyrical beauty:

Today I went into the hills. The sun was shining. I sat down beside a stream and a cow approached to drink. She had a good look in her eyes and I felt lonely.

'What is it like to be a cow?' I asked.

'Why should I tell you?' she answered politely, dripping water from her spongy lips.

'I'm writing a book and I'd like to record your point of view.'

'In that case,' she said, 'I'll tell you. Do you know the story of the wren and the mole?'

I was compelled to admit that I did not.

'Then the story of the grasshopper who fell in love with a water-lily – surely you know that?'

'Again, no.'

'Do you know why the little men in the grass are unable to eat barley?'

I shook my head.

'I can't explain anything to you,' she said, and walked quickly away to a tree which mounted her after the fashion of husbands. (p.16)

Throughout the book there is a strong sense of religious quest, but it is one filled with a deep sense of despair both of the quest itself and of a literature adequate for the times: 'Dying I see the house of the Redeemer go dark [...] There is no way to end this book. No way to begin' (p. 313).

It is true that alongside passages of great power and beauty there is some truly awful writing (as William Carlos Williams pointed out in a perceptive review of 1942). Nevertheless, more than seventy years on from its first publication, *The Journal of Albion Moonlight* remains as revolutionary and as pertinent as ever.

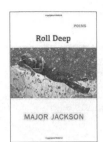

First and Third Worlds

Major Jackson, *Roll Deep*
(Norton), £12.99

Reviewed by IAN POPLE

Major Jackson's fourth collection *Roll Deep* is announced on the back cover blurb as 'A remixed Odyssey'. That sense of Odyssey is announced in the first poem of the book entitled 'Reverse Voyage'. In the poem, the narrator returns to what we assume is his home town, to 'the silence, oblique, hidden deep inside / the ventricle caves of my body's chambers, / to nail salons, check cashing stores, pawnshops.' This sense of place as something both embedded and embodied runs throughout this book; and these are places of return, or Other; cities and countries the writing explores.

That quotation, even found as early as it is in the book, is typical of much of the writing. Jackson impacts a lot into his sentences and his lines. The single verb 'hidden' pulls its subject 'silence' towards it and then the complements spin out behind it; although the subject is 'silence' the agent of 'hidden' i.e. who or what hides is, itself, hidden or elided. There is a subtle vowel music here as well. A Jackson line makes you work, and feels worked itself; these are words that need to be read slowly and dwelt on for their full effect to take place; which is, I would imagine, how Jackson would read the poems.

Thus, 'roll deep' might be a description of the aesthetic of this book; particularly so in the second section, 'Urban Renewal'. This part of the book describes Jackson's visiting Greece, Spain, Brazil, Kenya and Italy. These 'travel poems' work, to a great extent, in the way of much travel poetry in that the poems are as much a journey around the poet as they are journey in a 'foreign land'. Jackson's dense, impacted lines hoover up both image and impression and move quickly through the worlds these images evoke. This is also an emotional movement – 'Even here I look for / a history of myself' – as Jackson looks for black faces among the people illustrated in the 'frescoes, sculptures, altarpieces' and finds 'the slave boy delivering clothes to a nude Pollux,' and asks 'why every Christ child craves the adoration of a / black Magus: *shades frozen in a single hole.*'

Thus, a sense of a personal journey overlaid with an African-American diaspora permeates this book as a whole; the book is a kind of black Odyssey. And Jackson is brought up against the full force of this in the poem 'Tour of the Food Distribution Point, Ifo', where he witnesses the lines of the hungry waiting, in Kenay, 'for the First / of the Month like the poor in Detroit, a flea bite solution / in the fight against famine. We're stuck, our roles reversed.' Like the photographer caught in the war wondering whether to record or to help, Jackson is caught in that first world problem of not only travelling on a travel scholarship to witness the degradation of others and to record that witness, but also finding the relationship to his previous experience compromised. That Jackson succeeds in both that witness and working through that compromise is a testament to his technical abilities, as well as a deeper and enabling empathy.

Landscape or Language?

Jane Griffiths, *Silent in Finisterre* (Bloodaxe), £9.95

Reviewed by ALISON BRACKENBURY

Is it a matter of landscape or language?
the book asks. Where would you most like to live […] ?

The lives of Jane Griffiths' poems are intriguingly varied. The best work in her fifth collection, *Silent in Finisterre*, has startling freshness and power. Griffiths' sophisticated, unusually thoughtful poetry is often dominated by very early memories. Unashamedly, effectively, she repeats cherished place names – 'Taddyford', 'Gilgarran' – until they become part of her reader's mindscape. Some poems speak urgently to a lover, relative or friend. This may exclude readers, as in the haunted stories of 'The Museum of Childhood'. This sequence begins 'When you ask how I remember the past' and ends with 'nothing but seeing through'. I felt that Griffiths' vision was wonderfully seen through in her shorter poem, 'Revenant':

And I will go down to Gilgarran
        by sunset, cowbell, ice cream van
And I will go down to Gilgarran
        by myself, by name alone

Griffiths' technique can be compelling, not least through strikingly original rhythms. The lovely 'Song of Childhood' ends:

to range the sky that was tall as a crane
all the way to Starcross, and back again.

This airy couplet, in ten-syllable lines, hinges on lightly running syllables far closer to nursery rhyme than to iambic pentameter. The fluid spill of Griffiths' lines is particularly well-tuned to water. She listens to landscape with humble and perfect attention: 'Sure of itself, the sea said *Ahhh, ssshhh*'. (The lengthening of sound notation is both clever and exact.) Occasionally, last lines risk awkwardness through difficulties of sound and meaning: 'Here you couldn't only once think of home.' This can be challenging for readers.

Griffiths herself clearly relishes technical challenge, in bold exploration of varied landscapes of form. She does once wander offtrack, into a 'mirror poem'. A strong poet weakened is a good reason for a Reviewer's Rant. The all-too-common 'mirror poem' is a series of (usually) uninspired lines, repeated, still less inspiringly, in reverse order. It is chillingly good at expelling every ghost from its own machine. Treat each new poem as a struggling lamb. Do not sacrifice it on the altar of fashionable form!

But, although dulled by repetition, the reflections of Griffiths' 'mirror poem' include her acute opposition of 'landscape' and 'language'. Ideally, we could value both. But, as her question wisely suggests, we may have to choose. A reader might guess, without a biography, that Griffiths has been a lexicographer. Her poems refer frequently to 'language' and to specific literary terms: 'adjectival', 'anaphora'. Would the landscape of the following lines be more powerful without reference to a literary device?

What was it we were listening for [...]
                    metaphor before the word
metaphor, or our selves, the far side of the wall?

Griffiths' lines, with particular skill, often foreground a single exotic word, focusing on a detail in landscape: 'floreate', 'embowered'. This can be a source of delight to many readers, including me.

I particularly value Griffiths' leaps of language into wider, unexpected thoughts: new landscapes of mind. This is poetry which often works on suggestion rather than statement, as in the collection's final poem: 'The Question of Things Not Happening'. A shocking event is signalled by an uncommon word with a cold, sliding vowel: 'the road / elides to ice'. Delicate, falling rhymes from earlier stanzas haunt its last lines. Jane Griffiths' command of language is unobtrusive in a landscape perhaps of sorrow, surely of mystery and wonder:

And then, above the ploughed field,
birdsong. A weak sun. All calm
as if the girl might step unharmed
from her crumpled body in a world
where life carries on, like before.

As Broad As the Sun

Helen Dunmore
Inside the Wave
(Bloodaxe)
£9.95

Reviewed by SUE LEIGH

Helen Dunmore became an acclaimed novelist but began her writing life as a poet. Her work celebrates individual lives – often in dark times – and reveals a deep love of the sensory world. The poems in this, her last collection before her death, exist in the place where the human world meets what she calls 'the underworld'. Dunmore came to inhabit this territory because of serious illness. She describes it as 'a harsh terrain but lit up by its own intensity and luminosity'.

The sea is an important presence throughout. In the title poem, Odysseus returns to Ithaca to find he belongs to neither sea nor land, underworld nor living world. He goes down to the shore, turning his back to the land: 'on the inside / Of the wave he chose / To meditate endlessly [...] To watch it at eye-level, / About to topple / About to be whole'. To be alive, the poem suggests, is to travel within this place until the wave collapses and is gone. Odysseus in another poem addresses the ghost of the young Elpenor (who fell from Circe's roof as they were about to depart from her island): 'We had left you behind / But you are ahead of us / Waiting'. (Throughout the book, the living and the dead often walk together.) Dunmore frequents the classical world with ease and familiarity. 'The Place of Ordinary Souls' recalls the legend that unheroic souls pass their afterlife in the fields of asphodel. Dunmore counts herself among them:

'we dawdle / Towards the rumour of a beauty spot / Which turns out to be shut'. The contemporary, the lived present, is never far from Dunmore's vision.

This present includes her experience of being in hospital. 'Counting Backwards' considers the surprising opportunities offered by anaesthesia, the poem existing in the borderland between consciousness and unconsciousness, reality and what is imagined or hallucinated – here, the sound of a waterfall. In the ward, she likes 'the patter of cards / The lazy sandwich that falls open / Halfway to the mouth', then reflects, 'I used to think it was a narrow road / From here to the underworld / but it's as broad as the sun'. Dunmore often couples a mundane thought with a more serious one as if in the most difficult of times our essential identity is still there. A shaft of sunlight on her pillow and a quietness prompt: 'Who would have thought that pain / And weakness had such gifts / Hidden in their rough hearts?'

There are several poems that look back – like the *carpe diem* 'Hornsea, 1952' (the year of Dunmore's birth) which contemplates her mother's life: student days, marriage, children. 'Yes, but were we happy then?', the poem asks, 'all those cold days'. Another mother and children on beach holidays are recalled in 'The Duration' with its subtle undercurrent of sons lost in war (and its small shock at the end when we return sharply to the vivid present, 'There are hours yet. / Thousands, by her reckoning.'). Small scenes are vividly remembered – swimming in a blue pool, a visionary moment as a train stops somewhere on a plain, a snowy night alone with a new baby.

Dunmore's joy in the world – people, ideas, stories, art, nature – remained undiminished. As did her willingness to share it. 'Give me your hand / Onto the rock where the seaweed clings / And the red anemone throbs in its crevice / Through swash and backwash.

On a Naff Edge

Luke Kennard, *Cain*
(Penned in the Margins)
£9.99

Reviewed by NATASHA STALLARD

64–65
Reviews
Brackenbury
Leigh
Stallard
Muckle

The Genesis figure of Cain, who was condemned to wander the earth by God after the murder of his brother Abel, has appeared in the work of Byron and Titian and a Louis Armstrong song. In Luke Kennard's interpretation, Cain appears by ringing the doorbell, disguised by 'an actual size, inflatable Frankenstein's monster'. Cain becomes the antagonist, sidekick and spiritual guide to the narrator Luke Kennard – who is and isn't the same Luke Kennard as the author – as he tackles a crisis in faith, a marriage break-up, a hangover, a trip to a broken shrine and a festival performance at an 'unpopular poetry tent'.

Cain is Kennard's fifth book of poetry. The poems are linked by the narrative of Cain and Kennard's relationship, in a persona style similar to Ted Hughes' *Crow*, Jacob Polley's *Jackself* and Kennard's previous poem 'The Murderer'. Although not a radical departure from Kennard's usual tone of sad, slapstick and self-sabotaging characters, 'Cain' aims for more difficult and sincere subject matter than earlier collections *The Harbour beyond the Movie* (shortlisted for the Forward Prize) and *A Lost Expression* by examining the nature of faith.

Kennard, who was raised Protestant and is now Greek Orthodox, has described *Cain* as his most confessional work and his closest to language poetry. The book's centre piece is 'Anagrams', a series of thirty-one anagram poems, each only using the 335 letters from the story of Cain in Genesis 4:9–12. As a further constraint each poem outlines an episode of a TV show based on Cain, and is surrounded by a frame of tiny red text, in a similar tone to a DVD's director's commentary.

'Anagrams' is an ambitious strategy – the red ink is jarring to the eyes, the text jarring to the ears. Energetic and inventive, terms are overstretched to the absurd. Adah arrives via doorbell, just like Cain:

<Doorbell.> Adah in Burberry, bathed
in hall-light. Adah, rosebud torturer, co-
author of overset thermometers. Adah,
outshining hydrogen trinketry. Soothe
their wrathful orphanhood then come
hither, nutrient.

Kennard has previously praised an Amazon reviewer's description of his books as 'on the knife-edge of naff'. Using the constraints of anagrams and persona, *Cain* often feels as if it's revelling in its own naffness. It is intentionally jarring – placing us in a stream of boyish video games, zombie obsessions and corporate events, yet looking for God.

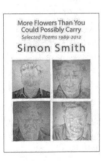

Alias Smith

Simon Smith, *More Flowers Than You Could Possibly Carry: Selected Poems 1989–2012* (Shearsman), £12.95

Reviewed by JOHN MUCKLE

Simon Smith is a contemporary English exponent of early post-war US poetics, and this career-spanning selected poems shows him always to have been a good poet. His edges are smooth and buff, his wit is sharp, and a brew based on the mixed grains of O'Hara, Spicer, Reverdy and Catullus is distilled into pure English moonshine. This book, edited by Barry Schwabsky, opens with a dense, politically-driven sequence in which he batters late capitalism to a pulp, quickly thereafter spiralling up into exquisite bird song, and soon develops a politicised lyric of domestic heterosexual happiness, which is the dominant mood of his writing. There's a *lot* of name-dropping: mille dedications to friends and contemporaries, copious references to poetic heroes and classics – a practice amounting at its most tiresome to a sort of obsessive self-positioning – but there is a genuine reverence for his chosen masters ('you knew all poets are liars didn't you, you knew' 'The Magician, Jack Spicer', p. 65) and warm affection for friends and poets who emerged just ahead of him in the late eighties. Lightness of touch is a prerequisite of the New York manner, and Smith's referentiality might have led to some soggy soufflés if he wasn't quite so astute, so wary of being caught out, and if his poetry wasn't also grounded in local cultural observations. Irvine Welsh gets a drubbing with a line referring to 'wankers from Crouch End who think *Trainspotting* is the real thing'. But this kind of louche inverted postcode snobbery and middle-class knowingness isn't all Smith has to offer, and he sometimes teases out a certain double-edged sympathy for his targets, here the populist view of poetry, that eludes heartlessness:

SENTIMENTAL EDUCATION

Thank you for handing back the neatly folded memories
thank you yes they were my fantasies thank you

yes they were mine and quite sentimental quite thank
you too you're right of course of course they were

too sentimental and they were mine
all mine and stunningly simple of course

thank you for the thirty boxes of dreams
sentimental full boxes full overflowing

sloping dreams over every side thank you

Simon Smith can write a Ted Berrigan sonnet as good as anyone's, but translation from more distant classics is also his forte. *More Flowers Than You Could Possibly Carry* is more or less framed by reworkings of Catullus and Martial, which nearly function as a bookends in this selection, the former an O'Hara-like celebration of sexual love, career-making ('I'll suck your pricks') and temporariness; the latter more valedictory, looking back on a gone life-world in which the best of times were those that were apparently frittered away:

But the state-of-play is neither's got it,
the good times sinking low as each sun sets.
So every day we loafed, chalked up as debts;
wouldn't every man live, if he knew how,
giving it all away to here and now?
('Martial, Book V Poem 20' p. 136)

Vigilant

Neil Powell, *Was and Is: Collected Poems* (Carcanet), £14.99

Reviewed by KEVIN GARDNER

In his title poem Neil Powell writes, 'I was the child who made a world in a shed; / Who talked to animals, birds and sunsets.' Solitude and loneliness are dominant themes in this collection, where nature, music and books often substitute for human encounters. Take the villanelle 'In a Cold Season': 'there are things half-heard / Across a world vacated by the word, / In this still dusk, this breathless interruption. / The resonant descant of a distant bird [...]'. Yet in a volume that goes to great lengths to establish the poet's isolation, Powell reveals many surprising human connections – in numerous poems addressed or dedicated to friends, in the recurring manifestation of 'we' and 'you', and in his journey to establish both poetic and personal identity.

Disconnection, however, is an unmistakable motif – or perhaps more properly it is the Forster-like uncertainty of human connection. In 'Gathering', for instance, Powell recalls participating in a poetry reading with John Mole and Peter Scupham. The poem's form (tercets in terza rima) implies a connective triad of poets, yet in his self-directed 'you' Powell disengages from the expected *we* of the three poets. He then 'banish[es]' the reader along with the listeners in his audience, reducing them to 'shades of philistines', though he equally disdains his own poems, 'as often loved as cursed'. Almost miraculously, the poem's tension and isolation melt into a spirit of concord and beauty: 'thus we trace // The narrow line which hovers in this place, / Encounter not art's seedlings but its bloom / And gather, pricelessly, some part of grace.' The unexpected expansion of rhymes adds to the experience of grace, for the poet and reader alike.

The mystery and depth of the world Powell moves in demands his imagination be expressed in formal structures. Thus *Was and Is* revels in quatrains and tercets, sonnets and villanelles, pentameters and hendecasyllabics; indeed, almost every poem of Powell's is an achievement in form. Heptasyllabic septets are on display in 'At the Edge', a poem that responds to humanity's insistent craving for answers: 'Through a vocabulary / which does what it has to do / with ungraceful exactness, / you express about the sea / things I shall never fathom, / confronting those mysteries / whose gift is their remoteness.' A Hungarian sonnet sequence, 'A Cooling Universe', counters the imperatives of death and the cold comfort of human memory: 'As time and darkness beckon us to sleep, / The curtain falls on all we could rehearse, / Hot fragments of a cooling universe.' In the face of time's 'cool indifference', Powell insists on the atoning consolation of art: 'At the poem's centre [...] [is] / The pattern of a world to be remade.' Out of this ordering impulse, 'We forge such fragments into monuments, / From ruins fabricate a world to last.'

That artistic pattern is often found close to home. 'For My Ancestors', a previously uncollected heptasyllabic poem, makes a vital connection between the poet and his familial past. Imagining the genetic origins of his personality and wondering 'what sort of men' he might have descended from, Powell asks whether they 'hid among trees / and tried to make some pattern / from the leaves'. If they too created artistic order and harmony out of the seeming randomness of nature, then, he concludes, 'I have inherited their / fear, solitude, and even / a little of their talent.' Powell avers that his natural trepidation and isolation contributed to the development of his own poetic inspiration: 'for I too must always hear / twigs snapping, the river run, / and the sound of evening birds.' If such is what *was*, it is no less what *is*.

Neil Powell's title calls to mind Peter Scupham's wry description of himself as one who 'regards "was" and "is" as words for the same thing, and [who] has an affection for that race whose verbs for the past are in the future, because, of course, they face the past and back cautiously forwards' (*The Rialto* 46, Summer 2000). *Was and Is* is the work of a poet who likewise moves tentatively forward by vigilantly studying his past. Powell's new collection embodies a thoughtful reconsideration and rearrangement of a fifty-year narrative of writing and publishing. The author has rejected a volume-by-volume arrangement in favor of a chronology of composition; he dispenses with some previously published poems and introduces a number of unpublished and uncollected pieces. This book is at once a valuable introduction to Powell and a brilliant reassessment of his remarkable career.

Changing Seasons

Katherine Gallagher,
Acres of Light (Arc)

Siobhán Campbell, *Heat Signature* (Seren)

Reviewed by JOEY CONNOLLY

Acres of Light by Katherine Gallagher is a 74-page warehouse of cliché: cliché of expression, cliché of form, cliché of thought. Nobody who spends much time reading poetry will find anything here they haven't heard several times before. In the first poem – set in a park in the summertime – there is a boy in the background 'on the sax', playing *Summertime*. And this is how the whole collection feels: for any object due to be described, the canonical expression of that object is reached for. Peacocks strut through halcyon afternoons underneath the azure sparkle of the sky. Love is fire: 'When your heart grips and won't let go, it's fire'. A love poem ends, genuinely, with 'happy ever after'.

It isn't just the phrasing that's hackneyed. The insights here seem to be that flowers in summer are nice, that it's sad when our loved ones die, that The Beatles wrote good songs. After a while you half expect a poem arguing that all unmarried men are bachelors. There's a lack of formal imagination, too: although mostly working in free verse, Gallagher seems to have 'had a go' at a bunch of well-known forms: there's a ghazal, a villanelle, a handful of haiku, a few tin-eared rhyming quatrains. The common factor is the total lack of indication that any thought has been given to the relation between the form and the content of a poem.

Of course, none of this is really a criticism. The fact that these poems have been included in places like *The Best Australian Poems 2012* (Black Inc), the *Daily Express* and *The Poetry Review* suggests that there's an audience and a taste for this kind of thing. So why bother reviewing it, given I'm clearly not the target audience – that I seem incapable of appreciating what the book's trying to do?

Well, usually I wouldn't bother. There are poems here, though, which aren't merely the harmless lyric-by-numbers I've been describing. There are several pieces which stray into the territory of the offensive.

One of these is called 'Quotidian', and is *'after a line by Mahmoud Darwish, "We love life whenever we can"'*. The Darwish poem is a short piece about the struggle of Palestinian people to find beauty in the world despite the oppressive conditions under which they exist – to love life when '[w]herever we settle we grow fast-growing plants, wherever we settle we harvest a murdered man.' Gallagher's response, though, twists Darwish's subtle, moving lines into a saccharine celebration of the uncomplicated joys of privileged Western lives, in which 'children gallop to school / clutching their frisbees', and the 'sun warms the butterflies' first flights'. The overwriting of Darwish – with no sense of the violence being done to his lines of complex protest – is grossly insensitive, both poetically and politically. To suggest that

Gallagher's experience of loving her life in which 'if we're lucky, we hear dolphins whistle / to each other' implies an ignorance of the lines she's repurposing.

There are other deeply questionable poems here – 'A Cautionary Tale', which uses the unattractive figure of 'Mildred' to chide women who wait too long before trying to have children; or 'Photograph – Mekong Delta, South Vietnam, 1965', about which the less said the better. Such poems forbid us to ignore the work. It's those moments in which the poetry becomes actively objectionable that make the book anything but entirely forgettable.

*

After all of which, Siobhán Campbell's book *Heat Signature* is a blessed relief. The work here is unflashy but restless; it refuses ever to shout its arguments, but neither will it fall entirely quiet. Most of the poems take Ireland and Irish politics or people as their subjects, but none are didactic, or hopeless, or aggressively decisive.

Campbell's book is a book of bare facts coaxed into a strange expressiveness by barely-perceptible atmospheres of loss, anger, danger or hope. Or any two or three of these at once. Take the poem 'In their high cheek bones runs the veins of a nation', which has a first stanza ending 'Even though their backs are bent with longing, / they may appear taller than they are.' In the next, a girl learns to be ambidextrous after a cruel teacher ties a hand behind her back. Later on, the poem warns against a 'creeping nostalgia' in the stories of those sent West during 'the Famine' and there 'caressed the oppressor's tongue'. These ambiguities of pride and suffering – of blame and self-acceptance – are played out in the poem's final two lines: 'An island passport might land you a tax haven. / Then again it could cost you an arm and a leg.', the grim literalism of the which is a good example of the mordant humour with which Campbell resists the idea of the Irish as subjects of English anthropological study.

Heat Signature is not entirely a book of quiet understatement, though. Take 'Tone', a lively roll-call of colourful metaphors for tone in its various forms, but also an Ars Poetica for Campbell. The following lines, as well as reproducing a favourite trick of hers – she's constantly forcing the physical to act as abstraction, and the abstract as concrete – also speaks to the way she's working to develop a poetics (and a tone) capable of talking about something as various and fractured as the Irish nation:

Nothing trumps tone but when there's a crack in it, watch
    what slips in.
It might be an anti-tone – undoing bravura, dulling the
    gloss, leaving tone spent,
in a fierce bad mood, exposed in the light of all that we
    once thought we shared.

Campbell's book has much to say – or, less than say: to evoke, to imply, to examine – about an Ireland enduringly shaped by an old conversation, including the conversation of poetry, about Ireland.

Questions and Answering Back

Harry Clifton, *Portobello Sonnets* (Bloodaxe); Emily Berry, *Stranger, Baby* (Faber); Anne Stevenson, *About Poems and how poems are not about* (Bloodaxe)

Reviewed by ANDREW HADFIELD

Harry Clifton's witty and engaging collection, *Portobello Sonnets*, is the latest offering from the distinguished Irish poet. Employing an epigraph from Patrick Kavanagh, 'In the third age, we are content to be ourselves, however small', the collection marks a confident and technically accomplished maturity, at ease with the ordinary stuff of life, as he returns to the Irish capital after sixteen years in Europe. The opening sonnets describe the poet's feelings to be back in a city at once familiar and strange in demotic language that is carefully crafted into sonnet form (Clifton varies his sonnets which are sometimes European and sometimes English in structure). The third sonnet describes snow in the early morning, and an empty scene as he looks out through his window: 'Listen, sit, be grateful for a day / When nothing happens. Time, pure light / And silence, the world looking the other way' (p. 11). Not only is this written in line with Kavanagh's epigraph but it is a telling reminder that nothing actually has to happen in a poem for it to be significant; or, indeed, enjoyable.

Sonnet 7 commemorates the life of an editor, the busy city alerting the poet that his verse has to do the work of memory because nothing will stop: 'New life, new continuities, now, at the end of our tryst' (p. 15). It is his duty to preserve the past, as he does elsewhere in the collection: 'They are holding the tram / As usual for Grandad, running late / From his job in the Tech, and Daddy with his plans / From the Corporation' (p. 40). But the Dublin he knew in his youth has changed and the city is now conspicuously multicultural. Tired and irritable on public transport at those around him the poet reminds himself that they have as much right to be there as he does, and starts to think like a host or guide: 'Eat on. Be grateful your place of birth / Is still your prison. Africans, Poles, Malays, / That's Camden Street outside there, in the rain' (p. 34). Even so, some things remain more or less the same. Woken from his reverie about the famous dead – Saul Bellow, the Pope – he sees a familiar figure, Pat Pomphrett, 'who can barely remember his own name', heading towards him: 'Lords spiritual, lords temporal, men of art / Protect me now, when the verbal shakedown starts' (p. 30). Again, the poet has to intervene as a recorder, as no one else will. *Portobello Sonnets* is a thoughtful collection, a potent reminder in its understated way that poetry often thinks biggest and best when it seems to think small.

Emily Berry's second volume, *Stranger, Baby*, is a very different beast. It is the place to go if you like your poetry loud, raw and confessional, rather than quiet, mature and reflective. This longish collection of lyrics is a painful response to the recent death of the poet's mother. Berry experiments with a variety of forms so that even flicking casually through the book one will see different layouts of words on the page: long lines, block capitals, a variety of spacing, single words in a row, split lines, poems that fill the page and ones that are only a line or two. There is a series of poems in the middle which reflect on the epigraph, Freud's statement, 'The loss of a mother must be something very strange.' These are the work's core and answer back to the great man in expressing a grief which is not easy to contain, explain or describe, showing him just how odd and discombobulating it is to lose a loved parent far too soon. Berry writes as if she is a therapist for Freud encouraging him to imagine a mother and a child climbing a hill 'as high as Leopoldsburg', where they find 'a kind of holy Sunday stillness over everything'. She tells him how to think ('You must imagine it like this'), following a long journey 'through the most desolate lagoons', then rather archly apologises for writing about such sad things. The poem conclude, 'To mourn [...] is of course permissible / On our way back it began to rain, but gently / The rest – you will know what I mean – is silence.' Citing Hamlet's last words to Freud would seem to be a way of making him realise just how true his statement is, and, one suspects, how insensitive Berry thinks the founding father of psychoanalysis has been to women (she may have his case study of Dora in mind). The problem a reader may have is that Berry is hectoring a reader just as much as she thinks Freud is, closing down any space for disagreement and exhorting submission to her voice. There is too much anger in this collection for it to work well, and the almost manic variety of the poems actually points out how similar so many of them are in tone and style. The long poem 'Ghost Dance' seems complicated as it morphs through various styles and changes, but it concludes like many other poems in the collection:

People can be removed from the world
They don't tell you that, but it's true
I mean, they do tell you, but they don't tell you
People you love can be removed from the world
(They can remove themselves)
They will be removed from the world
Didn't anybody ever tell you that

The repetitions and quirky use of the familiar which seemed fresh and original in *Dear Boy* are rather leaden and unimaginative in *Stranger, Baby*. Emily Berry is a poet of talent but needs to move on.

Anne Stevenson's *About Poems* is a collection of lectures on poetry given at Newcastle and Durham Universities. In them Stevenson talks/writes about what she thinks is valuable in poetry, interspersed with examples, and reflects on her long and varied career as a writer. Stevenson is often interesting but the lectures suffer from a lack of editing (there are repetitions which could easily have been ironed out) and her judgments can seem very familiar: 'A poem, if it is to be a work of art, must reveal, like a piece of music or a painting, emotional elements conveyed by sounds, rhythms and references that are untranslatable into any other form of language' (pp. 14–15).

In many ways, I suspect, this is a problem with the format.

However, Stevenson is endlessly fascinating when she writes about Sylvia Plath, the subject of the last lecture. Here she has something different to say and a controversial position to articulate and defend, because she is not an uncritical admirer. Stevenson respects Plath's technical skill as a poet but is less impressed with her representation of her self, her life and what sense she made of the world. Stevenson argues that 'Totem' and 'Words', two of Plath's last poems are 'perfect [...] but, as truth, they are sadly consistent with the plot of her personal drama' (p. 137). Stevenson argues that Plath was 'probably irrevocably damaged when, in the summer of 1953, sleepless and fearful of going mad, she was given, as an outpatient, electroconvulsive therapy' (p. 124), and she is far less hostile to Ted Hughes than many other critics. Not everyone will agree with her analysis, but anyone interested in Plath needs to read her.

What is the Wind Doing?

Robert Sheppard, *The Meaning of Form in Contemporary Innovative Poetry* (Palgrave Macmillan), £66.99

Reviewed by HILARY DAVIES

What is poetry? What is a poem? Is this a poem?

Well, it could be. It has both form and content. It uses a variety of tried and tested poetic devices. It scans. It asks questions, which some might consider profound, about how we use language to produce an effect in and on the listener; in latter centuries and amongst the literate, the reader also.

But we needn't stop there. You could, if you wanted, set it to music, sing it, project it onto a wall or some other flat surface, mould it in papier mâché or another medium of your choice, cast it in metal and even write it in water. You could tweet it, with a hyperlink to *PN Review*, perhaps. You could re-arrange the questions to highlight the emphases in a different way. You could ask a completely different set of questions. You could replace the word 'poetry' throughout with 'banana', or with 'pogge' or 'pogonic'. Or none of the above, but just think about having done them, and note how they change your attitude to the original poem. Or set of questions.

Now, these are neither team building away day ideas nor exercises in facetiousness. They, and analogous activities, crop up periodically in Robert Sheppard's collection of essays *The Meaning of Form in Contemporary Innovative Poetry*. Here's an example by Stefan Themerson, a riff on the children's rhyme 'Taffy was a Welshman', which Sheppard helpfully glosses for us as '(racist)' (brackets his):

Taffy was a male native of Wales
Taffy was a person who practised seizing the property of another unlawfully and appropriated it to his own use and purpose

The effect of replacing certain key terms with their dictionary definitions is of course first to amuse, then to distance, to ironise, to subvert. Themerson was an avant-garde film maker and children's book author; frequenter of the 1930s Parisian avant-garde; friend of Kurt Schwitters, Bertrand Russell, and Bob Cobbing; founder of the post-war avant-garde Gabberbocchus Press; and creator of the concept, 'Semantic Poetry'.

But he was also a Pole, a refugee from Nazi Germany, who had witnessed the collapse of empire and the horrors of two world wars. This list should be suggestive of who and what Sheppard's intellectual antecedents are; it reminds us as well, however, that the absurd, violent, arbitrary, surreal world that Themerson's work inhabits was only too grounded in reality.

Themerson's experiment also, as Sheppard acknowledges, antedates the linguistic juggling characteristic of the Oulipo movement. This movement is of central importance to Sheppard's category 'innovative poetry'. For 'innovative' in his hands is a classification, not a description, as we shall see. The roots of Oulipo extend in fact back to the formal experimentation of Rimbaud and Apollinaire, who are frequently invoked. But the actual name, derived from 'Ouvroir de littérature potentielle', appeared in 1960 out of a workshop series run by Raymond Queneau and others.

This is where our initial questions, 'What is poetry? What is a poem?' come in. For Sheppard, and for those he designates as 'innovative poets', poetry is about form, and Oulipo is a vital, though by no means its only, benchmark. Rules, or 'constraints', are at the heart of the Oulipean enterprise. This is in itself hardly new, since, traditionally, all poetry exists under some form of artificial constraint, even free verse. But it is here that we enter the arena of controversy. For the constraints that are imposed by this method are, in their origins, mathematical, algorithmic, a calculus with language, binding on the author who submits to it and yet, crucially, also arbitrary and cut loose from the constraints of the over-arching and synthesizing imagination of the author. At least in theory.

This is not surprising when you learn that many founder and subsequent members of Oulipo were, or are, distinguished mathematicians in their own right, making significant contributions in the areas of combinatorics, game theory and graph theory. To give you an example of what this might mean in practice: the rare words 'pogge' (a tiny, rather cute, spiny fish, native to Britain, with an upturned nose) and 'pogonic' (pertaining to beards) that I gave earlier, are examples of the Oulipo N +7 rule. That is, you have your original noun, in this case, 'poetry', and you substitute for it the noun that comes seventh after it in a particular dictionary; other criteria may be used to vary the counting, such as obsolescence. The most famous modern production from a related constraint, the lipogram, which is a form of wordplay already in use nearly two thousand years ago, is Georges Perec's novel *La Disparition*, written without using the letter 'e'. It's the sort of thing that appeals to both linguists and mathematicians, like a good game of language chess.

What are the implications of all this for poetry? Sheppard tells us, though not very succinctly or felicitously. Although he's keen to assert street cred through examples of innovative poetry that draw on post-punk, transcripts of harrowing rape trials, the hereditaments and detritus of a post-historic, post-modern world, this is all set within an intellectual context that gestures (a favourite word) towards the obvious Adorno, Barthes, Derrida and Benjamin, but also more recent theorists such as Derek Attridge and Jacques Rancière. His prose is full of modish and yet also hermetic academic speak, the puns, parentheses, Russian-doll syntax and uninitiated-excluding neologisms that characterise so much theoretical discussion in the humanities. Here we go: 'Dissensus (rather than consensus, both socially and artistically, in relation to heteronomy as well as autonomy) produces the manifold and broadly translational devices of formally investigative poetry (including the poetry now called linguistically innovative), but varieties of montage and de-montage emphasizing disruption, interruption, imperfect fit, and unfinish, as well as transformation and transposition – creative linkage in other words – put disorder at the heart of art's order, while simultaneously putting order at the heart of its disruptive practices.' (p. 236)

Well, who could argue with that? Joking apart, however, one of the more insidious effects of such writing is to pre-empt every possible point of dissent by the ubiquitous and inoffensive-looking copula, 'and' together with its equivalents, 'as well as' and 'both'. But a thing that can be everything risks becoming nothing. This is a pity, because underlying all the essays in this volume is a premise of the utmost importance, and even urgency. And that is that *form and poetry are inseparable.* This may sound obvious, but it no longer is. This is where Sheppard, and other such contemporary 'innovative' poets as Geraldine Monk, Jeff Hilson, Peter Hughes and Caroline Bergvall, all of whom he discusses in these pages, take issue with a lot of 'mainstream' poetry. He identifies a core philosophical divide, one which is probably even unconscious in those he regards as mainstream: that form matters, is dynamic, and inheres inalienably in the structure of poetry. This does not mean, as innovative poetry amply demonstrates, that form is necessarily reducible to set patterns, although he does devote one chapter to the sonnet. 'Form is not just a matter of technique, artifice, vessel, or conduit, [...] it is an active material force with semantic or cognitive value' (p. 17). He quotes approvingly from Lambros Malafouris, *How Things Shape the Mind: A Theory of Material Engagement* (2013) who investigates the organic relationship between maker and made; from this I think we can extrapolate also between reader and poem, and a poem and its form. Admittedly, two thousand years of thinking about this problem has not been able to come up with very many satisfactory answers, but that doesn't mean this relationship doesn't exist. Sheppard has it in for what he sees as the prevalence of a facile indifference to this fact: an alarming, amnesiac drift in much published poetry, and poetry criticism, towards only considering what a poem 'is about', towards the paraphrasibility of a poem: 'paraphrase is amnesia of form,' he quotes Angela Leighton as saying in *On Form: Poetry, Aestheticism and the Legacy of a Word*, (2007). And she, and he, are right.

This fissure is not recent, though the ubiquity of the workshop poem, so often, as it were, written by committee, by consensus as to what a poem is/ should be, has, perhaps, by its very spread, come to make such discussions seem irrelevant. But concern over the reification of poetry was the driving force behind modernism, Dada and surrealism; it was also behind the British Poetry Revival of the 1960s and 1970s, which sought to challenge what it saw as the pusillanimous aesthetic of the Movement. This culminated in the acrimonious turf wars of the late 1970s in the Poetry Society, when the then editor, Eric Mottram, a leading experimentalist, first Professor of English and American Literature at King's College, London and at that time editor of *Poetry Review*, was ousted from his post. After this, the schism deepened, with the two camps not acknowledging each other's existence for long periods since. As this volume demonstrates, the arguments have never gone away.

But how have they developed? The range of activities, and artists, covered in *The Meaning of Form in Contemporary Innovative Poetry*, exemplifies how diverse the paths are that a focus on form can take. They illustrate only too well that the temptation of form is to empty itself of meaningful content. Questions are begged: what is experimentation for if it becomes experimentation for experimentation's sake, and if the critical language used to describe it has itself become reified? Does this not now morph into its own orthodoxy? How oxymoronic is the perpetual revolution? What happens when an innovative movement in the arts moves into the academies, or even the commercial arena? These were not questions one necessarily had to ask of Bunting, Edwin Morgan, Barry MacSweeney, Tom Raworth or Tom Pickard, but they do need asking now.

And what of those who prize content over form? For whom the value of a poem is circumscribed by what it's 'about'? Where the coinherence of form is forgotten, which means, most worryingly, a forgetting that the nature of what is said is dependent on form. You *don't* say the same thing if the form of the language is different: only paraphrasable subject matter is the same.

One very big creative possibility is raised by *The Meaning of Form in Contemporary Innovative Poetry*: that we could conceive of a contemporary poetry that avoids the twin seductions of, on the one hand, a formalist experimentation swung loose from the lived life, and, on the other, a complacent 'narrationism' where the qualitative experience of the lives we lead is not transformed by the wroughtness, the artifice, the form with which we express it.

The poem is the cry of its occasion,
Part of the res itself and not about it.
[...]
said words of the world are the life of the world.

(Wallace Stevens, 'An Ordinary Evening in New Haven')

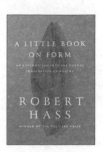

The Poetry Gym

Robert Hass, *A Little Book on Form:
An Exploration into the Formal
Imagination of Poetry* (Ecco);
Stephen Burt, *The Poem is You:
60 Contemporary American Poems
and How to Read Them* (Harvard)

Reviewed by TONY ROBERTS

There is a moment in *A Little Book on Form* in which Robert Hass offers his students (and now readers) 'a small exercise. Take an afternoon and reread Wordsworth's "Tintern Abbey" and "Immortality Ode" and maybe one other Wordsworth ode or the first book of The Prelude and Coleridge's "Frost at Midnight" and his "Dejection: An Ode" and then read – written about twenty-two years later, the five Keats odes – "Psyche," "Melancholy," "Nightingale,", "Grecian Urn," and "To Autumn."' One's first reaction is that this is a demanding workout – but there is a point to it: 'I don't know if you will share my experience of them, but I found that when reading them in that order, the striking thing about the Keats poems was that they seemed so beautifully finished and a little old-fashioned.' This sort of statement is characteristic of Robert Hass's critical writings. It combines insight, admiration and commitment with an open personal touch.

In this highly stimulating, though hardly 'little', book the acclaimed poet and essayist goes beyond metrical rules and rhyme schemes, to consider the 'formal imagination in poetry'. He is searching for a language to explore its intuition and creativity. Hence the tentativeness of 'notes toward' in the following: 'It seemed possible to construct notes toward a notion of form that would more accurately reflect the openness and the instinctiveness of formal creation'.

Mercifully this is not nearly as abstruse as it sounds. In fact, Hass offers quite a comprehensive course, developed to guide young poets at the University of Iowa Writers Workshop through two years of intense study. Beginning in 1995 Hass has added to these 'notes' which have swelled with the addition of so many examples of the poet's craft that *A Little Book on Form* offers an annotated anthology worth reading in its own right. In the interests of accessibility his approach has been to begin with consideration of the single line (the completed clause, the line, the one-sentence line, the one-line stanza, the experimental one-line poem) and then to move to the two-line poems and stanza, to three and then four (from which 'almost all the likely formal propositions in both metrical and free verse poems can be derived'). He turns then to blank verse (one 'implicit model' for free verse), followed by poetic forms (sonnets, odes and elegies, etc.) to end with consideration of stress and how free verse works.

What is on offer, then, is distance learning at the hands of a Berkeley professor, complete with frequent reading lists and occasional exercises. There is a great deal of information along the way: the synoptic history of forms; examples from different cultures (including Asian, Chinese and Persian); explorations of craft. Hass's students took their course in three hour sessions, the second half – student-led – on form outside poetry. Seasoned readers will work out their own timetable, attracted by old favourites from Horace to Heaney and the pleasure of discovery. (I might note that English poetry effectively disappears from consideration in the twentieth century. There are an honoured few outsiders: Breton, Lorca, Heaney, Herbert, Miłosz, Neruda, Yeats. Otherwise it's Americans from Whitman and Dickinson to, say, Lyn Hejinian and the poet's wife, Brenda Hillman.)

The book is commendable for its pithy explanations and insights: 'The term romantic is a convenience for observing a shift in the notion of the poem from the idea that the work of the imagination was to make vivid and attractive the ideas that are available to us through reason or an empirical common sense to the idea that imagination was not illustrative, but creative, that the imagination embodied its own kind of knowledge, deeper, phenomenologically fuller, than the kinds of thing the other labors of knowing afford us.' Discussing the ode – the longest and perhaps the most interesting part of the book – Hass turns to the inward journey of thought in 'Frost at Midnight', to the poem's structure: 'I wanted to call attention to this rivery movement in the verse of this period because it tracks a different sense of mind [anticipating surrealism and stream-of-consciousness] [...] It represents thought as something nearer to what we think of as imagination, a proceeding by intuitions having to do with likeness, with mirroring and echoing, with an oscillation between thought and sensation, discursive and mimetic modes.'

In an earlier essay, 'Listening and Making', Hass remembered a friend taking exception to a comment he had made about 'metrical inversion' in a line by Robert Lowell. 'He said he liked the piece well enough, but that one phrase – that finical tic of the educated mind – had filled him with rage.' Hass added, 'I think I understand why.' Perhaps the good-humoured *A Little Book on Form* isn't for his friend, but it should be for many of us.

While Hass's chosen poems have largely been tested by time, Harvard professor Stephen Burt has the difficult task of illustrating contemporary excellence (1981–2015). *The Poem Is You* is a celebration, from sea to shining sea, of the current state of American poetry. (I venture the patriotic touch because Stephen Burt sees poetry's health and especially diversity as an image of America itself.) He illustrates its vivacity in sixty essays, each following the poem which is its subject, explicating, contextualising, biographising and venturing into other fields in support: psychology, neuroscience, evolutionary theory, phenomenology and so forth. Diversity is certainly the key to the collection: 'the recondite and the demotic, the accessible and the challenging, mingle'. At the same time Burt repeatedly cautions that the chosen poems are only his take on the poetic variety to be found today. Thirty years from now, he suggests, the chosen poems might be 'in Spanish, or in Hmong, or in American Sign Language'. For less adventurous readers what is here may be confusing enough.

Although Burt does not make the point himself, he acknowledges that there are those critics like Marjorie Perloff who have long argued that 'models of poetry as conceptual exploration, resistant to speech, or perpetual experiment [have] replaced or displaced models of poetry as "lyric," or rendered it obsolete'. Certainly many of the poems in Burt's book are claiming or reclaiming what he likes to call 'space' from what had gone before (Zukofsky and Oppen, Lowell and Bishop). He defends Claudia Rankine's *Citizen: An American Lyric* (2014) as a bona fide recipient of poetry prizes as very sensible, 'if "poetry" means a text that brings together the many aspects of language in order to explore someone's, or anyone's, interior life, to challenge the transparency of common language, and to do something that mere exposition or narrative could never do'.

And so we have, in *The Poem is You*, an openness with forms – prose-sense deniers, a one-line poem, some computer speak, on-line alt-lit, a homophonic translation – but with common concerns and all, presumably, excellent. Burt's avant-garde choices are meant to open up questions of who is reading what and how we read it. Those gripping tightly to the lyric tradition may feel – using the old analogy of modern painting – that gallery walls alone confer status upon some of his chosen examples.

This is where Burt's admittedly excellent commentaries come to the rescue. He knows the poems; he knows the poet's background, techniques, and their public statements. He knows the poems that clustered around the one he chose for its representational nature. His method is to let us in on it all ('I chose this one because it shows how to read the others.'). Yet we may legitimately wonder at times if the ingenuity is in the poem or rather in Burt's exploration of it. Some of the chosen poems do not hold the reader's attention, or do not repay it. In these cases I felt – assuming I might be the mouldy fig – that an anthology served the poet poorly. Then again, shouldn't a poem be able to stand alone?

I seem to have fixated on the weaknesses of Burt's choices. Yet there are many excellent poems and poets too. There are highly informative essays on a number of poems by well-established poets like Miłosz, Ammons, Charles Wright and Komunyakaa, for instance. And there are memorable poems, like Merrill's 'Self-Portrait in Tyvek™ Windbreaker', Glück's 'Lamium' and C. D. Wright's 'Key Episodes from an Earthly Life'. I have had interesting introductions, too – to Linda Gregerson, Kay Ryan, Joseph Massey and Albert Goldbarth among others.

The Poem is You (shame about the title) compels serious attention as news from the poetry front. For that alone it would certainly be worth reading – and we have the extra benefit of Burt's enthusiastic ruminations.

—————————— COLOPHON ——————————

Editors
Michael Schmidt (General)
Luke Allan (Deputy)
Andrew Latimer (Production)

Editorial address
The Editors at the address on the right. Manuscripts cannot be returned unless accompanied by a stamped addressed envelope or international reply coupon.

Trade distributors
NBN International
10 Thornbury Road
Plymouth PL6 7PP, UK
orders@nbninternational.com

Design
Luke Allan
typeset by Little Island Press

Subscriptions (6 issues)
individuals: £39/$86
institutions: £49/$105
to: PN Review, Alliance House
30 Cross Street, Manchester
M2 7AQ, UK

Copyright
© 2017 Poetry Nation Review
All rights reserved
ISBN 9781784101480
ISSN 01447076

Type
PN Review is set in Arnhem, a typeface designed by Fred Smeijers in 1999.

Represented by
Compass Independent Publishing
  Services Ltd
Great West House, Great West Road
Brentford TW8 9DF, UK
sales@compass-ips.london

Supported by